UPON THIS ROCK
Biblical Principles of Church Planting
New and Revised

By

Bill Tinsley

Upon This Rock original publication
© 1985 Home Mission Board of the Southern Baptist Convention
William G. Tanner President
1350 Spring Street NW, Atlanta, Georgia

Upon This Rock New and Revised edition
© 2019 William Tinsley
The Tinsley Center
409 Peyton Dr.
Fort Collins Colorado
www.tinsleycenter.com

Scripture taken from the NEW AMERICAN STANDARD BIBLE
© Copyright The Lockman Foundation, 1960, 1962, 1963, 1968, 1971, 1972, 1973, 1975, 1977, 1995

FOREWORD

By Jeff Christopherson

You may not know it now, but you are holding something in your hands that might seem small, and unassuming, but is in fact wildly potent. Much like in year 2000, we could not have imagined the power and capabilities that could be stuffed into a three-by-five-inch slab of glass, plastic and silicon (that we now understand to be a smartphone), the book that you're holding may seem innocuous and unremarkable, but I assure you it is not. If you have an ear to hear the voice of the Spirit, a heart that craves God's hand on your life, and a passion for Jesus' kingdom to be revealed through your surrender – then you may just have found what your soul has been searching for.

Let me explain.

As I write this, I am travelling to a global church planting conference in Thessaloniki, Greece. Church planters from around the world will be gathering in the very city where Paul requested prayer that the "the Master's Word will simply take off and race through the country to a groundswell of response" – answers in themselves to Paul's prayer of faith. Heroic men and women happily paying unimaginable costs to bring the gospel to some of the planet's most unwelcoming geographies are gathering for encouragement, inspiration and mutual learning. As I consider how my words might support them as I envision the upcoming gathering in my mind's eye – words seem like such a small thing on my part.

As I literally ferry my way closer to the event, my mind travels back to time. How did a country boy from Prince Albert, Saskatchewan find his way here? How did a shy, introverted son of a welder make his way to be an encouragement to gospel missionaries in the very cradle where missions was born? How is it that I am able to experience this kind of grace? The answer to that question has everything to do with the book that is in your hands.

Here is what I mean.

It was 1986 and I was an optimistic, rosy cheeked graduate fresh from Southwest Baptist University in Bolivar, Missouri. Having long sensed a call to bring the good news to my homeland, I accepted a position to be a church planter in the oil-town of Lloydminster, Alberta. I was single, strategically clueless, had no local connections, but had a heart full of spiritual verve. I found a full-time job at a furniture store, and bi-vocationally began to plant the church which ironically would be named, Victory Baptist Church.

So, the twenty-one-year-old version of myself worked days at the furniture store, and spent evenings knocking on doors inviting people to a hotel conference room which was to be the home of a new church. Door after door, night after night, week after week, I found a polite yet sustained disinterest. I was fully expecting my obedience and faithfulness to translate into burgeoning baskets of spiritual fruit – but instead the lush, bumper crop that I had imagined was actually a dry, barren field. There were precious few successes to which I could point. I had to learn a whole new language to camouflage my ministry to others without tipping my hand that I was actually a ministry failure.

The vim and vigor that I started with began to leak badly. Embarrassment took the place of my former enthusiasm. The thought of spending a life doing this sort of thing seemed like the worst possible fate. Why did I tell so many people that God had called me to ministry? What was I thinking? I was deeply discouraged.

Thoughts of my father's welding shop began to preoccupy my thoughts. He had a thriving business that employed a dozen or so journeymen welders. I grew up in the business and knew it well and was confident that my dad would be happy to make room for me. I began to plot out my exit from ministry. I would have to employ my new spiritual language that equated faithfulness to fruitfulness, but I was mastering that already. I just had to get out.

My apartment in Lloydminster was a one-room bachelor suite. I didn't have a television, just a sound system with a record player, tuner, and a new cd player, and several bookshelves filled with what I once thought would become my tools of the trade. I loved books. I had shelves of bible commentaries, shelves of books on philosophy, especially twentieth century existentialism, and a shelf of books on ecclesiological subjects; church growth, Christian education, evangelism and outreach, and a couple of books on church planting.

My evening forays into the community as I expectantly knocked on doors became much more infrequent. Instead I spent most evenings, alone in my bachelor suite, listening to music and reading. If I had some books on "expanding your father's business," I would have enthusiastically read them – but I had none. So, I read what I had. Kierkegaard seemed to make me feel less miserable.

Sometime earlier, I was given a book called, "Upon This Rock: Biblical Dimensions of Church Planting" by William Tinsley, but it came too late in my church planting story. I had already emotionally checked out of the whole idea, so the book just sat on my shelf gathering dust. I didn't need another reminder of my failure. I had only two other books on church planting and had read both of those several times – and they didn't seem to help much. What could this book do?

But it was a small book. What could it hurt? So, I pulled it down from my shelf, pushed back my green vinyl recliner, and began to read.

And that was a mistake for the ministry exit plans that I was making.

All these years later I cannot remember which chapter grabbed my spirit and began to reorient my thinking away from personal failure and toward the faithfulness of Christ, but by the time I had finished the book, the Holy Spirit had done a number on me. The heavy burden of being unsuccessful in ministry had been lifted and was replaced with a new love for the One who had called me into ministry in the first place. No longer was I preoccupied with thoughts of escape, instead I began to re-imagine a life following Jesus. And what a joy it has been to live that life.

It seems difficult to conceive that from my inauspicious beginning into the world of church planting, that I would spend my entire adult life planting churches, planting churches that planted churches, leading church planting organizations, and now lead a church planting thinktank that influences over seventy denominations and networks across North America. God took the one thing that once caused dread, fear and discouragement and transformed it into a life's passion that has been sustained over a lifetime.

"Upon This Rock" is a statement of confidence, not in the strength and faithfulness of man, but in the unfailing goodness and power of Jesus Christ. William Tinsley was used by God to remind me of this simple truth, and that reminder changed the trajectory of my life.

Maybe God has a reminder for you. From my own experience, I would encourage you to read this book with caution. It may turn your life upside right.

Jeff Christopherson
Send Institute
August 2019

INTRODUCTION

In 1986 the Home Mission Board of the Southern Baptist
Convention published *Upon This Rock,* my first book on church
planting. I was 39 years old. Few people had a vision for
church planting and few books had been written on the
subject. I had planted my first church that planted other
churches and helped launch an effort with Texas Baptists to
start 2,000 churches in 5 years. A lot has changed since then.

The Home Mission Board became the North American
Mission Board, perhaps the smallest change among many. The
world changed. The digital age was launched and took flight.
Church planting movements swept South America, Africa and
Asia. The center of the Christian faith shifted from the
Northern Hemisphere to the South.

But some things remained the same. In particular, the Biblical
principles for church planting that I tried to identify have not
changed.

I have been gratified across the years by those who were
touched by my early efforts, especially Jeff Christopherson,
Chief Missiologist of the North American Mission Board.

I met Jeff about 15 year ago. He was the keynote speaker for a
mission conference in Atlanta. We met in a buffet line, across
from one another. He saw my name tag and asked if I had
written a book entitled, *Upon This Rock.* I said I had. He said
that book changed his life. He had been discouraged with his
early efforts at church planting and was thinking of leaving the
ministry until he read my book. Somehow God used it to
rekindle a vision. The rest is history. God is using Jeff to
change the world.

I have seen some of the concepts put forward in my early effort resurface in more recent church planting books. Most of those, I expect, took place because the principles of church planting are universal. Sooner or later, those who are serious about the effort come to similar conclusions. I would like to think that some of those early seeds took root, sprang to life and bore fruit in others.

The 1986 publication of *Upon This Rock* is out of print. I suppose there are a few dog-eared copies circulating around in used book stores. But, other than that, it is not available. After meeting Jeff and stumbling across a reference to his experience with *Upon This Rock* in Dino Senesi's book, *Sending Well*, I decided it was time to revise and rewrite it.

I have learned a lot in the last 33 years. I have visited churches and church planters on six continents. For eight years I gave leadership to churches and church planting in Minnesota and Wisconsin. I am currently working with church planters in northern Colorado. Illustrations, applications and some of the content in my early book needed updating. So, here it is. I hope you find it helpful.

I am not sure how the passion to plant a church that plants other churches took root in me. Perhaps it happened when I was 19 preaching youth revivals in Oregon and Washington. Perhaps it took place in Indiana when I helped plant a church as a summer missionary when I was 20. Perhaps it came from the missions DNA of First Baptist Church, Corsicana, Texas, the church where I grew up. That church was born out of the church planting movement that swept Texas in the late 1800s. Noah T. Byers was the founding pastor. He had been the munitions officer for Sam Houston during the Texas Revolution. After Texas independence he planted churches across Texas along with Z. N. Morrell and R.E.B Baylor and many others. In 65 years Baptist churches multiplied from 1 to 3,000.

Whatever the source of that passion, my wife and I both were convinced God was calling us to plant a church that would plant other churches. So, in 1975, I graduated with a Doctor of Ministry degree from Southwestern Seminary in Fort Worth and resigned my position as pastor of the Franklin Baptist Church in Franklin, Texas. We left a 100-year-old county seat church to start a new church north of Dallas with 7 members. I was 29.

God was good, as always, and blessed us. I made many mistakes. There are many things I look back on that I would have done differently. But the church grew to more than 400 in attendance and planted two other churches in seven years. The rest of the story is too long to tell in an introduction, but you get the idea.

I am grateful to have witnessed God's movement on the earth in my lifetime. I am grateful for the wealth of resources now available to church planters and the leaders that God has raised up with vision for church planting movements. I hope God will use this revised edition of *Upon This Rock* to encourage you to accomplish His purposes on the earth.

Bill Tinsley
Fort Collins, Colorado
2019

TABLE OF CONTENTS

CHAPTER ONE

A TIMELESS STRATEGY

Twenty centuries have passed since Jesus gave His command: "Go therefore and make disciples of all the nations" (Matt. 28:19). Nearly a hundred generations of Christians have run their life races, each passing to the next this flaming mission mandate. Encouraging advances have been made in the last few decades, yet the completion of the task remains far from sight. In 2010 the Gordon Conwell Research on Global Christianity estimated 32.8% of the world's population is Christian. The Pew Research Center agrees with this, estimating total Christians at 1/3 of the global population.

The Christian faith made significant inroads in South America, Africa and Asia in the closing decades of the 20th century. The center of Christianity has shifted to the global south. Philip Jenkins, in his book *The Next Christendom,* described the typical contemporary Christian as a woman living in Nigeria or in a Brazilian *favela.* Nevertheless more than two-thirds of the world's population remain outside the saving grace of God in Jesus Christ. Fully half of the world's 7.7 billion people have never heard the name of Jesus.

We must ask ourselves, what does God intend? Is He content with a "reasonable percentage" of the world's population to name the name of Jesus as Savior and Lord?

It seems clear that Jesus had something else in mind when He commissioned His disciples. It is His passion that all men and women of every nation come to faith in Him. Surely He intended that this command, of all his commands, should be obeyed and fulfilled. "The Lord is not slow about His promise, as some count slowness, but is patient toward you, not wishing for any to perish but for all to come to repentance" (2 Pet. 3:9)

Every time Jesus gave a command, He provided the means for that command to be obeyed. When He commanded the lame to walk, atrophied muscle and sinew, bone and nerve sprang to life. He who had been carried on a pallet not only stood to his full stature but was able to take up his own bed and walk" (Luke 5:24-25). His command to the deaf to hear resulted in sound stimulus previously unknown to those silent senses (Mark 7:32-35). When he commanded Peter to step from the boat, he provided firm footing on the watery wave (Matt. 14:29).

In all of Scripture Jesus never gave a command He did not intend to be fulfilled. And in all of Scripture, God provided the means by which the commanded could obey. When it comes to the Great Commission of Matt. 28:19-20, we can only conclude that Jesus both intended that this, His greatest command, should be obeyed and that He provided the means for its fulfillment.

So why has the church fallen short? Where has the Christian movement gone wrong?

Each generation has marshalled new strategies and manufactured arsenals of spiritual resources to carry out Christ's command. With sword in hand, some have fielded whole armies, launched great armadas and led bloody Crusades to Christianize the world. Some have retreated into monastic solitude, fleeing temptation and forging fortresses of moral purity. Others have hoped to convert the world using mass circulation of the printed message. The 15th century invention of the printing press enabled dissemination of the written word to homes and farms. During the Reformation, God's message moved all Europe with paper sails on rivers of ink.

Still others have looked to education as the strategy to fulfill the Great Commission. Colleges and Universities have been founded throughout the world so that young and old, rich and poor, might discover for themselves the Kingdom truth.

At the close of the 20th century strategies took an increasingly technological turn. I purchased my first PC in 1982, a Commodore 64 with 64k of memory. It used machine language and a 360k floppy disc. I used it to write the first edition of this book. Ten years later the internet was introduced. At the dawn of the 21st century, social media swept the world. The gospel went digital.

Each generation of believers has employed innovative strategies in an effort to fulfill Jesus' commission to make disciples of all the nations of the earth. But what is the one strategy that will succeed? It seems incomprehensible that Jesus would lay before His followers such an awesome goal and not, at the same time, give them the strategy to achieve it.

His changeless strategy is found in His statement to Peter, "Upon this rock I will build my church and the gates of Hades shall not overpower it" (Matt. 16:18).

Jesus made this statement at Caesarea Philippi. I have visited this location twice. He was about to make His final journey to Jerusalem where He would lay down His life. Before doing so, He led his disciples far to the north, away from the Jewish authorities, away from the crowds. He wanted time to prepare them for the things that were about to transpire. After feeding the multitudes, Jesus led His disciples on a long trek northward to the Lebanon border.

The area was known for its lush gardens and the Banias spring that gushed from a huge rock face, the source of the Banias river that flowed into the Jordan far north of the Sea of Galilee. It was an ancient site for Greek and Roman idolatry, dedicated to the worship of the god Pan. A temple had been carved out of the rock. Its features remain to this day.

It was here that Jesus introduced the pivotal conversation, "Who do men say that I am?" When he made the question more personal, "Who do you say I am?" Peter responded, "You are the Christ, the Son of the living God." At this point, with the pagan rock cliffs forming a backdrop, Jesus made His strategic statement. Within this statement lie the dynamic, the design and the dimensions of His strategy to fulfill the Great Commission.

The Dynamic of His Strategy

The dynamic of his strategy is divine, supernatural: "*I* will build *My* church.*" Often as much significance lies in what Jesus did not say as in what He did say. In this case the significance lies in the fact that He did not say, "*You* shall build the church." His emphasis is clearly on the first person, "*I* will build *My* church.

This dynamic is integral to the very nature of the church. The church is not a human institution that can be explained only in terms of sociology or philosophy. Any attempt to examine the church strategy in terms that ignore the divine is inadequate. The church has been infused with the creative agency of Christ from its beginning. He whose nature it is to initiate and create says of the church, "I will build."

Without this divine dynamic, the church degenerates into a mere social institution with little to distinguish it from the United Way, Kiwanis, or Lions Club. All are effective and needed institutions, but none claim a divine dynamic.

It is perhaps in this area that the world most frequently questions the church. Is there something in the church that cannot be found anywhere else? Is there a divine presence?

4

Quite clearly the church has made progress toward fulfilment of its purpose – to disciple all nations – only when this dynamic has been present. Of that initial expansion within the church at Jerusalem, much is attributed to the fact that "everyone kept feeling a sense of awe; and many wonders and signs were taking place through the apostles" (Acts 2:43). This sense of the spiritual dynamic at Jerusalem continued to be fueled by the healing of the lame beggar at the temple gate (Acts 3:6-8), the prayer meeting following the threat by Jewish authorities (Acts 4:24-31), the sacrificial giving among the Christians (Acts 4:32-37), and the miraculous release of the apostles from prison (Acts 5:17-32). Without this sense of God's presence, growth of the church at Jerusalem would scarcely have occurred.

The remainder of the book of Acts reveals the significance of this divine power in church planting at Antioch, Cyprus, Lystra, Philippi, Thessalonica, Athens, Corinth and Ephesus. Can churches be expected to grow in great numbers and to impact the lost world on any other grounds? Certainly not! But how can this take place?

Christians must recognize God's movement in the world, in the church and in individual lives. Too often His activity goes unrecognized. It is dismissed as "men drunk with wine at the third hour of the day" (Acts 2:15).

It is astounding that so many Jewish and Gentile leaders could ignore the intervention of God in Jesus' day, dismissing the miracles and defending the status quo. Today's generation may be guilty of the same. What has been called commonplace may be the activity of God, and what is viewed as a threat to established organizations and traditions may be evidence of His Spirit. We must cultivate an eye for the divine dynamic.

God must be depended upon to send an outpouring of His Spirit. The true moving of the Spirit of God within His churches cannot be manufactured by programs and technique. The significant moments when God intervened to alter the course of history were not moments fashioned by human hands. Peter had no concept of the journey that lay before him when he accepted Andrew's invitation (John 1:40-42). Saul of Tarsus had no idea of the dramatic turn his life would take when he set off for Damascus (Acts 9). Martin Luther could have never predicted the course his life would take when lightning struck him to the ground.

When God moves in the lives of men and women, He leaps denominational lines and eclipses every manmade strategy and program. Not every generation experiences such a moving of God's Spirit, but it is happening in our lifetime.

Phillip Jenkins and others testify to the fact that the mushrooming movement of new believers in South America, Africa and Asia is characterized by a conservative belief in the Bible as God's authority for life along with supernatural demonstrations of God's power including visions, dreams and healing.

The Design of His Strategy

Jesus' design for his strategy is the church, the *ekklesia:* "I will build my *church.*" The apostles embraced the church as the pivotal cog through which the power of God would transform the world.

If we removed everything in the New Testament related to planting and growing churches we would lose almost everything following the Resurrection. The book of Acts is devoted to events and circumstances surrounding church planting. It traces the early beginnings of church planting from Jerusalem, to Samaria, Antioch, Macedonia, Greece and Rome.

The letters of the apostle Paul (Romans, 1 and 2 Corinthians, Galatians, Ephesians, Philippians, Colossians, 1 and 2 Thessalonians) are all occasioned by planting churches in those strategic cities. From them we glean a wealth of material regarding doctrinal and practical foundations for new churches. Add to the list the pastoral letters to Timothy and Titus, since they were converts in the church planting process. These include instructions to church planters for effectively planting and growing healthy churches. Peter's letters were addressed to those in "Pontus, Galatia, Cappocia, Asia and Bithynia" (1 Pet. 1:1). James to the diaspora. John's letters and Hebrews were circulated among the churches. The book of Revelation is addressed to the churches of Asia Minor, all of which were established by implementing Jesus' strategy.

To remove church planting from the New Testament would, in effect, remove all Scripture beyond the Gospels. It is clear that the early disciples adopted church planting as their strategy to penetrate the first century world.

Jesus' strategy offered flexibility. He did not devote great portions of His teaching to create exact blueprints for the development of His church. As it grew, the church developed offices for leadership, instruction, administration and ministry, as well as music and liturgy. Along the way they found places to meet. Jesus did not see these aspects as definitive of his strategy. He avoided organizational structures that could not adapt to changing cultures. He refused to reduce His design to brick and mortar.

The book of Acts and the Pauline letters demonstrate no concern for property purchase and building construction. The first century followers of Jesus did not focus on buildings to define the presence of the *ekklesia*. Careful research of the Scriptures reveals only a blurred image of meeting facilities for the first century church. They mostly met in homes.

Our contemporary Western world suffers from an over-identification of the church with buildings. Church buildings on corners of major thoroughfares offer a false sense of security. The cities appear to be "churched," yet millions are untouched by the gospel and the support of a church family. In many communities gleaming white church spires rise above rooftops while cross-tipped shadows fall upon oblivious multitudes.

Don't get me wrong. Buildings can be helpful and useful as places to assemble and equip the body of Christ. But buildings, in and of themselves, do not define or create the church.

The design of Jesus' strategy creates a people distinguished by their "called out" relationship to the Father. Without a new nature, followers produce organizations and structures doomed to the same corruption that grips the socio-political structures of the world. But as people experience transformation, whatever varied structures, operations or organizations they employ can be in-breathed with redemption.

His design is couched in terms of people. Its simple form is two-fold: people in relation to God, and people in relation to people.

People in relation to God

Ekklesia presupposes a "calling out." The term is a binding of two Greek terms, *kaleo,* meaning "to call" and the preposition *ek* meaning "out." It reflects the literal experience of people being "called out" into assembly by a given signal: a trumpet, bells or vocal shouts. In Jesus' design love of God is supreme in the lives of those who are "called out." The difficulty arises in loving God as He truly is.

8

Most men love God "made in their own image." To the degree that image is challenged, chipped or fractured, they resist, even to the point of violence. The key is to love God so supremely that He shatters and shapes all those preconceived images into a sharper image of Himself.

The process of conforming to the image of God can be painful, difficult and confusing. The book of Acts reveals a people whose God was coming into sharper focus and consequently shaping their lives. The assumption that God could be fully known in a mere lifetime – let alone a few short decades – is the height of presumption. The character of His "called out" people will not exhibit pompous boasting of ultimate knowledge of God, but humble submission in a supreme love of Him that is open to new discovery of His person and presence.

People in relation to people

His design is also for people to love one another as they love their very lives. Jesus' focus upon this essential characteristic is unmistakable: "A new commandment I give you, that you love one another, even as I have loved you. By this all men will know that you are my disciples, if you have love for one another" (John 13:34-35). Jesus did not conceive of his *ekklesia* apart from this love. Without love for one another, the church ceases to exist.

So great was the quality of this love among the disciples that the church begins its expression with all members holding all things in common. Even the murmuring among the members in Acts 6 is evidence that selfless care for one another was the expected expression of the church and that the lack of care for the entire fellowship was intolerable.

In too many instances the church has demonstrated its ability to build buildings, develop budgets and fill calendars, but in the end has produced only sounding brass and clanging cymbals. While churches may exist with many organizational structures, a variety of music and liturgy in diverse accommodations, the church cannot exist without a sense of *agape* and *koinonia* among its members. *Agape* is the unconditional love of God. *Koinonia* is the unique relationship between believers that includes honesty, transparency, authenticity, generosity and love.

Christ's design for His church is not just believers in relation to believers, but believers in relation to non-believers. If His design for the church were to turn totally inward, believers focusing on themselves, the church would smolder to ashes rather than ignite a flame of compassion and redemption transforming the hearts of men and women. His imagery is clearly one of aggressive redemption: "the gates of Hades shall not withstand its onslaught" (Matt. 16:18). Against all other devices, the gates of Satan's stronghold remain unscathed, but against the irresistible force of the church, his gates shudder, giving way to the masterful advance of Christ's body.

Jesus' metaphors of "salt" and "light" go to the core of *ekklesia*. (Matthew 5:13-16). Though each of these elements have different characteristics, both salt and light are able to penetrate. Salt penetrates the substance in which it is placed; the smallest light penetrates and dispels the darkness.

To conceive of Jesus' strategic design apart from evangelism is impossible. If the Son of Man came to seek and save that which was lost, then His body, the church, must be doing the same. The church finds its reason for being, not in providing a sanctuary for those already saved, but in compassion, sacrifice and bold penetration of the darkness with the message of Jesus Christ that those who are lost may be saved.

People of weakness

That the design of Christ's strategy should be accomplished through people presents a paradox. How can the ideals of ultimate love for God, sacrificial love for others and redemptive love for the world be carried out by men and women who fall short in their love for God, who are more concerned about themselves than others, who feel fearful and inadequate for the task? It appears the church is defeated before it has begun. How could Jesus fail to take into account the flawed humanity that would doom His design to mere dreaming?

Those who were nearest Jesus were convinced that Jesus knew in His spirit what men were thinking (Mark 2:8). He knew that the spirit is willing and the flesh is weak. Certainly Jesus did not develop his design for the church with a blind eye to flawed humanity.

The church is composed of men and women who – like Lazarus from the tomb – bring with them decaying grave clothes that carry the stench of death. As a result, churches are made up of men and women who relate to one another at varying degrees of spiritual maturity and carnal weakness. At times the church rises to its zenith showing devotion, love and redemption. At other times it descends to the depths, expressing hostility, prejudice, envy and self-centeredness. Like those humans who compose it, the church has infinite capacity for the divine and the demonic.

. ....

A study of Paul's letters reveals that the early church struggled with this paradox. The first century church at Corinth was ensnared in jealousy and immorality. Paul did not hesitate to publicly confront the cliques forming around personalities; nor did he gloss over the immorality that the church was tolerating (1 Cor. 5). Neither did he fail to address the fact that fellow believers were dragging one another into civil court over property disputes.

The church in Galatia was in a doctrinal tailspin, "deserting Him who called you by the grace of Christ, for a different gospel" (Gal. 1:6). They had given in to the traditions of Judaism and built again a legalistic approach to salvation. Paul also indicated disharmony among the members when he wrote, "The whole law is fulfilled in one word, in the statement. 'You shall love your neighbor as yourself.' But if you bite and devour one another, take care lest you be consumed by one another" (Gal. 5:15).

He exhorted the Ephesians to put away the practices of their pre-Christian lives: sensuality, impurity and greed. Theft and falsehood were to be replaced with diligent labor and honesty. His exhortations reflect the tensions within the Christian community.

Perhaps this contrast between divine potential and human weakness is best demonstrated in Jesus' statements to the seven churches of Asia Minor as recorded by John in the book of Revelation. The Ephesians' remarkable perseverance and endurance was offset by their departure from their first love. Smyrna's spiritual wealth in the midst of physical poverty would be tested by arduous persecution. Pergamum's commendable refusal to deny the faith while under Satanic pressure contrasted with its tolerance of the teaching of Balaam and the Nicolatians. The church at Thyatira accomplished greater deeds than ever before, yet it was tolerating immorality. Sardis enjoyed a great reputation among the church and the world, but underneath its glamorous exterior was inner spiritual decay. Philadelphia demonstrated little power, yet before it stretched almost endless potential. Laodicea achieved "financial freedom" – demonstrating the economic power of the gospel – but was lured into lukewarm apathy, trusting in financial strength while becoming spiritually blind and poverty-stricken (Revelation 2:1-3:22).

This paradox is sharpened by the limits of mortality. Saintly men and women who have seen horizons unknown to the rest, are silenced by the grave and replaced by younger, less experienced believers. Every generation must rediscover faith. If God is to work in this generation to accomplish His purposes He will work through weak flesh.

This is the design of Jesus' strategy: churches conceived with love for the Father, sacrificial love for one another and redemptive love for nonbelievers, locked in a carnal struggle with imperfection. His design is a "divine treasure in earthen vessels" (2 Cor. 4:7).

The Dimension of Jesus' Strategy

The dimension of Jesus' strategy is life and death. "The gates of hell shall not prevail against it." The precise word in Matthew 16 is *Hades*, the realm of the dead. When Jesus adds, "I give you the keys of the Kingdom. Whatever you bind on earth shall be bound in Heaven," He is underlining the fact that this is *the key*. This is His strategy! However you employ this strategy makes a life and death difference.

The church was conceived by Jesus because of the heavy gloom hanging over the human spirit and suffocating mankind's highest ambitions for life and peace. Sad, indeed, it is for people to live in a world of moral and spiritual darkness, where nightmarish phantoms of lust, greed and selfish indulgence are released without restraint. But sadder still is the human spirit that lives unaware of the darkness that engulfs it without yearning for a new light to dawn. It is to those who cry out in abhorrence of evil and lift their heads in pursuit of righteousness that Jesus said, "Upon this rock I will build my church."

Jesus accurately perceived and portrayed the spiritual darkness in which this world is gripped. It is the darkness of death.

Without Christ, without the cross, all humanity is under the sentence of death. We are "condemned already" (John 3:18). "Death has passed upon all men because all have sinned" (Rom. 5:12).

In Christ alone is the hope of life. Peter's confession is discovery of this hope. The church possesses the keys of life and death as the gospel is proclaimed and men and women are discipled.

Quite apart from a creeping darkness that lengthens its shadows into a world of diminishing light, Jesus saw a world under a dark cloud of death. Into that darkness He introduced a light that lays bare the sinister and treacherous presence of the evil one.

Too often the church has been viewed as a sanctuary for retreat from an evil world. Too often Christians have hid behind stained glass windows attempting to drown out the cries of an anguished world with their music.

It is Satan's stronghold that is threatened. The foundations of his doomed kingdom quake at the advance of the church. His citadel is under siege.

The dimensions of Jesus' strategy includes every strata of society from those with political power to the poor and weak. It includes every ethnicity, every language and every culture. The church is equipped to penetrate every segment of humanity.

Rick Warren stated, "The single most effective method for fulfilling the Great Commission that Jesus gave us is to plant new churches! Two thousand years of Christian history have proven that new churches grow faster, and reach more people, than established churches. The growth on any plant is always on the newest branches." [1]

Questions for discussion:

1. Is our church experiencing the dynamic presence of God? Is there a sense of God at work among us? How is this demonstrated?
2. Is our church committed to the Great Commission? What are we doing to spread the gospel?
3. What is the key strategy envisioned by Jesus and practiced by the apostles to accomplish the Great Commission?
4. Am I allowing God to shape my image of Him or am I clinging to my own image of who God is?
5. Does our church demonstrate *agape* love and *koinonia* fellowship? How are these demonstrated?
6. What are positive attributes of our church that will enable it to achieve its potential?
7. What are obstacles that would hinder our church from fulfilling its potential?
8. Is our church retreating from the world trying to survive, or are we penetrating the darkness with the message of light?

---

[1] Ed Stetzer and Warren Bird, *Viral Churches* (Josey-Bass, 2010) Introduction.

CHAPTER TWO

MULTIPLICATION

The 21st century is fueled by multiplication. This is evident in population growth, technological expansion and financial investment.

The number of human beings continues to multiply, taxing resources for food, housing and employment while adding pressure to environmental concerns. When I entered church planting in the mid-1970s the world population stood at approximately 4 billion people. That number has almost doubled to today's estimate of 7.7 billion. The United Nations projects global population to reach 9.8 billion in 2050 and 11.2 billion in 2100.

Apollo 8 launched the day I married my wife in 1968. On Christmas Eve, we watched Frank Borman and his crew disappear behind the moon for the first time and listened as they read Genesis 1. Like Apollo 13, they used a slide rule on board for quick calculations. My children have never heard of a slide rule, much less used one.

I entered the digital age in 1982 when I slipped into Toys R Us under cover of darkness and bought a Commodore 64. From there I graduated to a Compaq portable with two floppy drives costing $2,000. I installed my first hard drive and discovered the computer was more transportable than portable, more like a heavy suitcase.

Mobile phones required the trunk space in a car. Then came bag phones, followed by mobile phones that looked like a brick. They could be used as lethal weapons. Today I converse with Alexa, Siri and Google. Artificial intelligence and self-driving cars are not just the wave of the future. They are here. Cyber-attacks are more feared than nuclear weapons. The technological revolution continues its exponential growth.

Multi-million dollar empires continue to be built by those who know how to multiply their investments. When Benjamin Franklin died in 1790 he left $5000 to each of his favorite cities, Boston and Philadelphia with the stipulation that the money be invested and the interest compounded for 200 years. By 1990 the $5,000 initial investment had grown to $20 million. As Franklin said, "Money makes money, and the money that money makes, makes money."

We live in an exponential, multiplying world. Here lies the problem with the current church strategies: we are employing the wrong mathematical function. We are attempting to penetrate a multiplying world with simple addition.

Adding (and subtracting) Disciples in a Multiplication World

Every year, churches are *adding* new converts to the kingdom. Most will baptize approximately the same number of persons baptized the year before. Most of this increase is erased by attrition, the loss of members through death, mobility and drop out. As a result, the vast majority of churches experience a plateaued attendance, and many experience decline. Few actually record net growth year to year.

Even mega churches are limited to growth by addition. If they baptize several hundred people in a single year, they are likely to baptize the same approximate number the following year. If average attendance increases by a few hundred, which is rare, it will not likely increase by more than that number the following year.

This principle holds true for churches of any size. Each church baptizes approximately the same number it baptized the year before, and most churches average approximately the same attendance they averaged the year before. With the churches that exist today, growth will consist of addition at best. The church is structured to add disciples rather than multiply them. Existing churches cannot build fast enough, nor adequately expand their organizations, leadership and assimilation structures to multiply disciples.

Churches, as a whole, remain relatively small. In its report on the status of faith in America in 2016, the Barna Group pointed out that most American Christians attend churches with fewer than 100 in attendance (46%). Only 8% of professing Christians attend mega churches of more than 1,000 attendance and only 1% of churches ever grow to 1,000 or more.

In 1982 the Southern Baptist Convention (SBC) reported 36,302 cooperating churches. As of 2018, the SBC reported 47,522 churches. Southern Baptists have added 11,220 churches in 36 years. At the same time the U.S. population grew by 96 million.

The Assemblies of God U.S. attendance grew by 787,558 between 1980 and 2017.

United Methodists (UMC) reported an average weekly attendance of 2,749,926 in 2016 after annual losses of more than 50,000 attenders per year each year since 2002.

The Presbyterian Church USA has been in decline since the 1960s with large losses between 2012 and 2016. Instead of focusing on new churches, the denomination has focused on numbers of churches dismissed averaging more than 100 per year since 2012. In 2017 the PC(USA) lost 67,714 members and 147 churches.

According to Pew Research Center there are currently 51 million Catholics in the United States, a decline from 24% to 21% of the population between 2007 to 2014. A report by Gallup in April 2018 noted that fewer than 4 in 10 Catholics attend church in any given week. The report noted that "those 21 to 29 are less likely than older adults to identify as either Protestant or Catholic. This is partly because more young people identify as "other" or as other non-Christian religions, but mostly because of the large proportion – 33% -- identifying with no religion." [2]

By its nature, it is difficult to come up with any verifiable numbers regarding non-denominational churches. We have to rely on big picture summaries from such research groups as Pew, Gallup and Barna.

The Pew Research Center stated in May 2015, "The Christian share of the U.S. population is declining, while the number of U.S. adults who do not identify with any organized religion is growing. … While the drop in Christian affiliation is particularly pronounced among young adults, it is occurring among Americans of all ages. The same trends are seen among whites, blacks and Latinos; among both college graduates and adults with only a high school education; and among women as well as men." [3]

Gallup notes that the percentage of Americans who claim no religious identity has more than doubled from 7% to 18% since

---

[2] Gallup, Lydia Saad, Catholic's Church Attendance Resumes Downward Slide, April 9, 2018
[3] Pew Research Center, America's Changing Religious Landscape, May 12, 2015

1991 while those who claim religion is very important has declined from 58% to 51% over the same period. [4]

According to Barna, " If an individual meets 60 percent or more of a set of factors, which includes things like disbelief in God or identifying as atheist or agnostic, and they do not participate in practices such as Bible reading, prayer and church attendance, they are considered post-Christian. Based on this metric, almost half of all American adults (48%) are post-Christian."[5]

Multiplying Disciples in the Early Church

The American experience of churches being plateaued, declining, or, at best showing slight increases in numbers of disciples stands in stark contrast to the first century church. The book of Acts opens a window on the phenomenon that multiplied disciples so that within three centuries the Roman Empire was saturated with churches and followers of Christ.

At first the church stumbled out of the starting blocks. Three thousand were added to the number of believers at Pentecost, only 50 days after the resurrection of Christ. But there was no effort to carry the message beyond Jerusalem. Instead, the followers of Christ hunkered down and settled in, waiting for his eminent return. It took an external force – persecution -- to launch the first century followers on a global quest for new disciples.

After Stephen was stoned to death, with young Saul of Tarsus aiding the mob that attacked him, a fierce oppression was unleashed on the nascent church in Jerusalem. Many believers fled. "And on that day a great persecution arose against the

---

[4] Gallup, Frank Newport, 5 Things To Know About Evangelicals In America, May 31, 2018
[5] Barna Group, The State of the Church 2016, September 15, 2016

church in Jerusalem; and they were all scattered throughout the regions of Judea and Samaria, except the apostles" (Acts 8:1).

With the apostles firmly rooted in Jerusalem, the common believers ran, with Saul of Tarsus in hot pursuit. "Saul began ravaging the church, entering house after house, and dragging off men and women, he would put them in prison." (Acts 8:3). They ran to familiar places: to Samaria, to Caesarea Maritima, to Damascus and to Antioch. And, where they ran, they told others about Jesus and formed small communities where new believers could worship, encourage and instruct one another in the faith.

The result was a widespread awakening in Samaria. "Therefore, those who were scattered went about preaching the word. And the multitudes with one accord were giving attention to what was said" (Acts 8:4-5). "When the apostles in Jerusalem heard that Samaria had received the word of God, they sent Peter and John" (Acts 8:14.) Far to the north non-Jews were coming to faith in a place called Antioch. "So then those who were scattered because of the persecution that arose in connection with Stephen made their way to Phoenicia and Cyprus and Antioch speaking the word to no one except to Jews alone. But there were some of them, men of Cyprus and Cyrene, who came to Antioch and began speaking to the Greeks also, preaching the Lord Jesus. ... And the news about them reached the ears of the church at Jerusalem, and they sent Barnabas off to Antioch" (Acts 11:19-22).

It is noteworthy that the explosion of faith and churches across Samaria and Syria was not coordinated from a central authority. The apostles were simply responding, as best they could, to what they were hearing. The movement had a life of its own. It was ahead of them and they were struggling to catch up.

Part of that life soon took flight on the feet of Saul, the transformed persecutor of the church. Much time had elapsed since he enabled the murder of Stephen and set out to track down followers of Christ in Damascus. A confrontation with Jesus had changed him and he had eventually found his way home to Tarsus, dazed and waiting for whatever God had in store.

Barnabas found him. It must have taken some time and effort for Barnabas to locate Saul. There was no quick form of communication, no cell phones, no internet, no social media. Barnabas set out on the long journey from Antioch to Tarsus to find him. Somehow he sensed that in this place, where Greeks were coming to faith, the converted persecutor might be useful. After all, he was eloquent in Greek and acquainted with the Roman world as well as Judaism. Barnabas brought him back to Antioch. (Acts 11:25-26).

The story from that point is well documented in the book of Acts. "And while they were ministering to the Lord and fasting, the Holy Spirit said, 'Set apart for me Barnabas and Saul for the work to which I have called them.' Then, when they had fasted and prayed and laid hands on them, they sent them away" (Acts 13:2-3).

Their effort on the first missionary journey sputtered. Going where they were most familiar, they set sail for the island of Cyprus. It was Barnabas' birth place. While they witnessed God's power at work and saw the proconsul, Sergius Paulus, come to faith in Christ, there is no evidence that they planted a church. John Mark abandoned them and returned home.

By the time they reached Perga of Pamphylia, Paul and Barnabas realized they would have to change tactics if they wanted to make disciples. They would need to plant churches. This they did at Antioch of Pisidia, Iconium, Lystra and Derbe. (Acts 13-14). By the time they returned to Antioch Saul's name had been changed to Paul and they had a firm grasp on the church-planting strategy Jesus had given them to disciple the nations.

It is at this point that the early church leaders in Jerusalem made a crucial decision. How much control would the Jerusalem fathers exercise over the expanding movement? What kind of restrictions would they employ? James, the half-brother of Jesus, had become the Jerusalem leader and he spoke for the rest when he concluded, "It is my judgement that we do not trouble those who are turning to God from the Gentiles, but that we write to them that they abstain from things contaminated by idols and from fornication and from what is strangled and from blood" (Acts 15:19-20). This they included in a letter to the new Gentile believers and concluded, "If you keep yourselves free from such things, you will do well. Farewell" (Acts 15:29).

It is hard to imagine a more minimal requirement. The fathers at Jerusalem refused to set up centralized control with lengthy tests for conformity. They essentially gave their blessing with a few practical instructions and let them go!

Paul's second journey with Luke, Silas and Timothy went further. After visiting the churches established in the first journey, Paul and his companions headed West, following God's vision and concentrating on metropolitan centers that could influence entire regions: Phillippi, Thyatira, Ephesus, Corinth, Thessalonica and, eventually, Rome.

From these centers the gospel spread, churches were planted and disciples were multiplied. Paul captured the movement like this in his letter to the Thessalonians, "For the word of the Lord has sounded forth from you, not only in Macedonia and Achaia, but also in every place your faith toward God has gone forth" (1 Thess. 1:8). And to the Corinthians, "Knowing that He who raised the Lord Jesus will raise us also with Jesus and will present us with you. ... that the grace which is spreading

23

to more and more people may cause the giving of thanks to abound to the glory of God" (2 Cor. 4:14-16).

The book of Acts captures only a small segment of the church planting movement that transformed the first century world. Acts focuses on the activities of Paul and his companions. But there were many others. Peter addresses his first letter to those who are in Asia and Bithynia, regions Paul was not permitted to enter (1 Pet. 1:1; Acts 16:6-7). Someone else carried the gospel to Asia and Bithynia and planted churches.

At the same time churches were penetrating to the south and east as far as India. Josephus, the historian, noted that churches were starting so rapidly that they could not be counted. The first center of Christian learning was established in Alexandria, Egypt and the great theologian Augustine emerged as bishop at Hippo in North Africa by the close of the fourth century. In spite of intense waves of persecution the church continued to spread like salt and leaven throughout the Roman Empire. In less than 4 centuries Christianity had become the official religion of the Roman Empire.

Multiplying Disciples In Our Day

There have been other times that churches have multiplied and Christianity has expanded at an astonishing rate. None, perhaps more prolific than the last few decades. This may come as a surprise to some. Many view Christianity only in terms of what they see in the United States and Europe. If that is our only measure, we would conclude that the Christian faith is in decline. If we examine what has occurred in the Southern Hemisphere we find a different story.

According to the World Christian Database the number of Christians in Africa grew from 10 million in 1900 to 493 million in 2010. In the same time frame, the number of Christians in Asia grew from 22 million to 352 million while the numbers in Latin America grew from 62 million to 542 million. The number of Christians in Africa is expected to double again to 1 billion Christians by 2050.

Phillip Jenkins' book *The Next Christendom* is perhaps the best resource on this astounding spread of the Christian faith. He states, "The era of Western Christianity has passed within our lifetimes, and the day of the Southern churches is dawning. The fact of change itself is undeniable: it has happened and will continue to happen." [6]

This rapid expansion is fueled by the multiplication of churches in the global south: South America, Africa and Asia. Jenkins states, "These newer churches preach deep personal faith and communal orthodoxy, mysticism and puritanism, all founded on clear Scriptural authority."[7]

They are missional and evangelistic. "Moreover churches on all three continents share a passionate enthusiasm for mission and evangelism that is often South-South, organized from one of the emerging churches, and directed toward some other region of Africa, Asia or Latin America – we think of Brazilian missionaries in Africa, Ugandans in India, Koreans in the Middle East." [8]

In the 1990s David Garrison described the explosion of Christianity in the global South in his book, *Church Planting Movements*. According to Garrison, Southern Baptists stumbled across this remarkable movement of God when David and Jan Watson filed their missions report recording a hundred towns, villages and cities in which new churches had sprung up with thousands of converts.

---

[6] Philip Jenkins, *The Next Christendom, the Coming of Global Christianity*, Third Edition (Oxford University Press, 2011) p 3.
[7] *Ibid. p 9.*
[8] *Ibid. p 16.*

An intense examination unearthed a startling discovery. Church planting movements were spreading spontaneously in Africa, Asia and South America. Garrison writes: "During the decade of the 1990s, Christians in a Latin American country overcame relentless government persecution to grow from 235 churches to more than 4,000 churches with more than 30,000 converts awaiting baptism."[9]

"A missionary strategist assigned to a North Indian people group found just 28 churches among them in 1989. By the year 2000, a Church Planting Movement had erupted catapulting the number of churches to more than 4,500 with an estimated 300,000 baptized believers."[10] According to Garrison, a Church Planting Movement is *a rapid multiplication of indigenous churches planting churches that sweeps a people group or population segment.*[11]

In many cases, these churches look little like our western churches. Instead of focusing on buildings and budgets to pay salaries for clergy, these churches meet anywhere they can assemble, often in houses, store fronts, even under a tree. Their pastors and leaders are volunteer. Often with limited education. When their small space is full, which can happen quickly, they start a new church meeting wherever they can. New pastors and leaders are recruited and discipled by those who are more mature.

According to China Digital Times, "Despite the ongoing crackdown, house churches are expanding rapidly across China. The growing role of home churches is in some instances spurred by government suppression itself as worshippers seek

---

[9] David Garrison, *Church Planting Movements, How God Is Redeeming a Lost World* (Monument,CO, Wigtake Resources, 2004) location 177
[10] *Ibid.* location 186
[11] *Op cit.* Garrison, location 245

alternative venues to continue hosting religious services. In Henan, for example, parents are gathering in private homes to bring services to their children following a ban on minors from entering churches." [12]

Instead of seminary degrees and ordination, they look for the qualities Paul sought: "For the overseer must be above reproach as God's steward, not self-willed, not quick-tempered, not addicted to wine, not pugnacious, not fond of sordid gain, but hospitable, loving what is good, sensible, just, devout, self-controlled, holding fast the faithful word which is in accordance with the teaching, so that he will be able both to exhort in sound doctrine and to refute those who contradict (Titus 1:7-9).

The Secret to Multiplying Disciples

The secret to this rapid expansion of the Christian faith is **begetting.** In the same way that human population has grown exponentially, so it is with churches and the Christian movement.

When churches give birth to churches, a multiplication factor is set in motion. Below is a chart for one church and how the "begetting" process works. It does not represent a Church Planting Movement, as described by David Garrison. This example is only exceptional in the sense that most churches never give birth to another church. But when any church engages in starting other churches, it can have a significant effect. I chose this church "family tree" because it was part of my experience. This chart is reproduced from the original publication of my book in 1986.

---

[12] China Digital Times, *China Continues Crackdown on House Churches.* September 11, 2018.

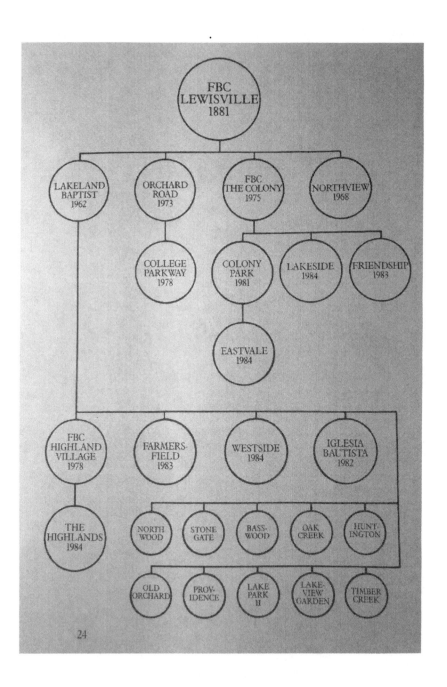

FBC
LEWISVILLE
1881

LAKELAND
BAPTIST
1962

ORCHARD
ROAD
1973

FBC
THE COLONY
1975

NORTHVIEW
1968

COLLEGE
PARKWAY
1978

COLONY
PARK
1981

LAKESIDE
1984

FRIENDSHIP
1983

EASTVALE
1984

FBC
HIGHLAND
VILLAGE
1978

FARMERS-
FIELD
1983

WESTSIDE
1984

IGLESIA
BAUTISTA
1982

THE
HIGHLANDS
1984

NORTH
WOOD

STONE
GATE

BASS-
WOOD

OAK
CREEK

HUNT-
INGTON

OLD
ORCHARD

PROV-
IDENCE

LAKE
PARK
II

LAKE-
VIEW
GARDEN

TIMBER
CREEK

24

28

The "mother church" in this story, is First Baptist Church, Lewisville, Texas which was started in 1881 as part of a church planting movement that swept across Texas. Only 1 Baptist church existed in Texas in 1835 with about 50 members. Over the next 65 years Baptist churches in Texas multiplied to over 3,000.. Z.N Morrell captured this movement in his book, *Flowers and Fruits from the Wilderness,* published in 1882.[13] On the eve of his 80th birthday, Morrell reflected: "Under the providence of God I have lived to see one preacher multiplied into 1,800, one church into 2,100 and less than 50 Baptists into 120,000."[14]

The diagram on the opposite page is a snapshot of the church planting that grew out of that church between 1962 and 1986. It started with First Baptist Church enlisting Jim Angel to plant Lakeland Baptist Church in 1962. In 24 years the combined attendance grew from 200 (the attendance at First Baptist in 1962) to over 3,000. Since 1986 over half of the churches in this diagram have closed, but the churches that still exist, along with others they started, have grown to reach many more thousands.

We are always grieved when a new church dissolves. But attrition is part of the powerful force in nature's multiplication process. A robin recently built her nest outside our window. She remained on the nest for weeks, never seeming to move. Always vigilant. Always alert. Smothering the eggs with her warmth, she waited patiently until her babies cracked open the thin blue shells that surround their embryonic beginnings. Only 25% of baby robins survive. But they are one of the most common birds in North America. Jesus' parable of the sower reflects the reality of attrition in the process of multiplication. We should never hesitate to start churches for fear they will

---

[13] Z. N. Morrell, *Fruits and Flowers from the Wilderness* (Commercial Printing Company, 1882; Baylor University Press, 1976)
[14] *Ibid.* p. 412.

not survive. Even those with short life spans often touch and change lives.

First Baptist Lewisville relocated in the 1990s and grew to more than 1500. I was interim pastor at the church when they voted to purchase land to relocate from their limited space in downtown. Stephen Hatfield led them through the relocation and continues to serve as their pastor.

But my part in the story centered on First Baptist The Colony. In 1975 FBC Lewisville invited my wife and me to start a church with seven members meeting in a fire station. It was the only public building in the unincorporated community of starter homes. At 29 I resigned my position as pastor of a 100-year-old county seat church and embarked on planting a church in what became The Colony, Texas.

The church grew rapidly. Two years later, convinced we could not reach people fast enough, we called David and Brenda Bird to plant Colony Park Baptist Church. A few years later Colony Park sponsored Lakeside.

Several African American families became part of our church. In 1982 a few of these asked if we would help them start their own church. They wanted a church that embraced traditional African American worship and organization. We agreed to help.

A small dying church on 121 offered to donate their property to our church. Camey Baptist Church had been started a century before when there was a small community by that name. The community had vanished. Only a few families still attended the church and none of them lived nearby. We agreed to accept the property and start an African American church in the building. They named it Friendship.

30

The first pastor was a failure, playing white interests against black. After he was dismissed, we found Paul McBride, an African American bi-vocational pastor who worked for the telephone company. The church grew.

We continued to receive black families as members at First Baptist. But Friendship provided a worship style far different than our own. Rev. McBride remained as the pastor for many years and eventually retired. The church relocated into The Colony and grew to more than 1,500 in attendance.[15]

We were able to move a mobile home into The Colony in 1976 to provide temporary space for weekday ministry. We quickly launched a Mothers' Day Out program to serve the many young families that were relocating from Iowa, Indiana and other northern states. After constructing our first building in 1977 we moved the mobile home into Highland Village where our good friends, Monte and Beverly Martin started First Baptist Church, Highland Village.

FBC Highland Village grew slowly. But Monte was able to lead them to purchase land and construct their first building. They grew to about 80 in attendance. Monte left to take a position with Southwestern Seminary. The church called another pastor. Ten years later the church still averaged less than 100 and, again, needed a pastor. By that time I was serving as Director of Missions for Denton Baptist Association. I agreed to serve as their interim pastor.

I sat at the back of the room during business meeting one night as the church spent 20 minutes debating whether to replace the warming element in a coffee pot. I told my wife, "This church will never grow." In 2002 the church was again looking for a pastor. They asked me to preach. They had grown to about 200 and built a new worship center. It appeared they were

---

[15] Web site for Friendship Baptist Church, The Colony www.fbtc.net

turning a corner. I had no idea what a big corner they were about to turn. They called Matt Chandler and changed their name to The Village Church. [16]

The church exploded with growth and planted churches in Frisco, Keller, Coppell and Bryan-College Station, Texas. They relocated and created the Village Church Network in Flower Mound, Denton, North Dallas, Fort Worth, Plano, and South Lake, Texas. The Village Church averaged 10,030 in attendance in 2014.[17]

In 2012 Matt Chandler was appointed President of the Acts 29 Network and the Acts 29 headquarters were moved to The Village Church. In October 2018 the Acts 29 Network reported 730 churches on six continents. According to their web site, the Acts 29 Network "exists to encourage, resource, facilitate, support and equip churches to plant churches that will plant church planting churches!" [18]

Whenever churches plant new churches amazing things happen. God is able to surpass our wildest dreams and imaginings. He can and will surprise us in the least expected places. Ed Stetzer and Warren Bird stated in their book, *Viral Church,* "We believe that we are on the edge of seeing an exponential multiplication movement [of church planting] in the United States." [19]

We have already seen a remarkable increase in the numbers of young men and women who feel called to plant new churches. It is on the rise. I am currently working with nine church

---

[16] https://thevillagechurch.net/about/history
[17] https://thomrainer.com/2014/07/2014-update-largest-churches-southern-baptist-convention/
[18] www.acts29.com
[19] Ed Stetzer and Warren Bird, *Viral Church* (Josey-Bass, 2010). Loc 250, ebook.

planters with new church starts in the Fort Collins area of northern Colorado. They are passionate, talented and gifted men and women. Three of these churches launched January 2019 and each of them have expressed a vision for starting other churches.

Questions for discussion:

1. How did our church start? Did another church sponsor the start of our church?
2. How old is our church?
3. How does the average attendance at our church today compare with the average attendance of our church 10 years ago?
4. How many people are added to our church each year?
5. Is our church growing by addition or multiplication?
6. What is the population of our community?
7. How does the population in our community today compare with the population 10 years ago?
8. How could our church move from mere addition to multiplication of disciples?
9. How many daughter churches has our church sponsored?
10. How many daughter congregations could our church sponsor in the next 10 years?
11. Could our church become the parent church of another church this year?

CHAPTER THREE

VISION

"When he saw the vision, we concluded God called us to preach the gospel to them." (Acts 16:10)

This was Paul's second mission expedition. The first had been a steep learning curve. He began as Barnabas' assistant at Cyprus, Barnabas' and John Mark's homeland. Their witness had been effective. The proconsul, Sergius Paulus had come to faith in Christ, but they failed to plant a church. This changed at their next stop in Pisidian Antioch. By the time they returned to Antioch, they had planted churches at Iconium, Lystra and Derbe and appointed elders in each place.

He was anxious to visit these churches again with his new companions. After a brief falling-out with Barnabas over John Mark he had taken Silas for the journey. Along the way he added young Timothy and the Greek physician Luke.

After encouraging the churches established on the first effort, he was ready to launch out to other regions. But where? They considered going into Asia, but the Holy Spirit forbade them. They then sought to carry the gospel into Bithynia. But, again, the Spirit of Jesus said no.

How the Holy Spirit communicated this to Paul, we don't know. It could have been an audible voice. God clearly spoke to Paul on at least two other occasions. But this time it appears to have been an inner voice, a feeling inside, a sense that these were not the right destinations. God often guides His followers in this way.

At Troas the question was settled. In the night Paul saw a vision, a man of Macedonia begging them to travel to the West and help them. When Paul told his companions, they were all convinced. Luke writes, "When he saw the vision, immediately we sought to go into Macedonia, concluding that God had called us to preach the gospel to them." The vision was pivotal. The vision would sustain them through many difficulties and discouragement.

Others would go to Asia. Still others would carry the gospel to Bithynia, places that Paul never entered. When Peter wrote his letters he addressed them to "those who reside as aliens scattered throughout Pontus, Galatia, Cappadocia, Asia and Bithynia" (1 Peter 1:1). God had a vision for others to carry the gospel into these regions. But His vision for Paul and his companions was to the west, to Philippi, Thessalonica, Berea, Athens and Corinth.

Effective church planting needs a vision from God.

I am not speaking about a physical vision, one that we see with our eyes, though this can happen. I am speaking of an inner compulsion, a sense in the heart, soul and mind, that this is where God wants us to go. This is where He wants us to plant a church.

Throughout most of my life I have had a habit of a morning devotion: a time for Scripture, meditation and prayer, often times at sunrise, usually outside. I have not been perfect. I have missed some mornings. But I have found this practice life changing on many occasions. In Minnesota and Colorado I have bundled up in sub-zero weather and taken my place on our deck, watching the sunrise, listening to God.

On an autumn morning in 1992 I was praying on the patio behind our house in Denton, Texas. I don't remember the Scripture or the subject. But I remember God said to me, "I want you to explore whatever I bring into your path." The words were not audible, but the message was clear.

I had not been open to going anywhere. I was serving as Director of Missions for Denton Baptist Association. We were focused on starting churches in the fastest growing county in Texas. We had recently started a church in our home.

Within a week I received a call from Becky Dodson in Wisconsin. Becky's parents-in-law had joined the church we started in The Colony, Texas in 1976. When Becky and her husband came to visit his parents, they attended our church and she remembered me from those many years before. She told me the executive director for Minnesota Wisconsin Baptist Convention was retiring and she was on the search committee. She asked if I would consider moving to Minnesota.

I said, "Becky, I have already made that decision. I have already told the Lord I would consider whatever he brought into my path."

Within weeks my wife and I were on a plane to Minneapolis. We met the committee in Rochester. Neither of us had every visited Minnesota or Wisconsin. But it was October and the landscape was awesome: hills ablaze with autumn colors, a cool nip in the air.

They decided to bring us back for a second visit in December. Things had changed. The streets were buried under four feet of snow. The temperature might have reached zero for a high that day.

After our visit, we sat at the Rochester airport waiting for our return flight. It was snowing – sideways. They were clearing the runway, blowing snow 30 feet into the air. They announced they were de-icing the plans. I peered out the windows into the storm and saw visions of Dr. Zhivago stumbling out of the frozen tundra, bleary-eyed with a frozen beard.

I turned to my wife sitting by my side and said, "What do you think?"

She said, "I think God is calling us here."

That's the way visions from God work. He plants a seed that grows into a passion and a calling.

When I told our friends in Texas that we were going to Minnesota they looked at us as if we were crazy. They said, "It's cold in Minnesota!"

I agreed. But, I said, "I have been looking for that passage in the Bible and cannot find it, 'So send I you to favorable climates not too far from home.'"

For the next eight years we devoted ourselves to planting and serving churches in the Upper Midwest, one of the great joys of our life where we continue to stay connected and involved.

...

Chuck Friemel grew up in Louisiana and became an air traffic controller. Caught in the Air Traffic Controller crisis in 1981, he was forced to find a new career. He went to seminary. Upon graduation he felt a strong call to Minnesota to plant a church.

Chuck and his wife, Susan, flew to Minnesota and met the Director of Missions responsible for church planting in the southern third of the state, a region that stretched from Wisconsin to South Dakota, from Iowa to the Twin Cities. The Director had a list of places that needed a new church. He pulled it out and started to describe all the options and possibilities.

Chuck listened patiently and then said. "We will be glad to look at any place you want, but God has called us to Red Wing."

Following God's vision, Chuck and Susan moved to Red Wing, Minnesota, a picturesque town overlooking the Mississippi River, the home of Red Wing Shoes and Red Wing Stoneware. Chuck found a job in an ice skate factory and signed up to play goalie on a local hockey team. He couldn't skate well, but he could block a puck.

Chuck and Susan started the Hiawatha Valley Baptist Church in 1990. They met in the Twin Bluff Middle School until November 1995 when they built their first building. Chuck and Susan followed God's vision and planted their lives. Today Chuck is the longest tenured pastor of any church of any denomination in Red Wing, Minnesota.

...

I met Paul Berthiaume in 1993 when I moved to Minnesota. He was in his early twenties, newly married to Whitney, a delightful young couple in Superior, Wisconsin. Paul grew up in Superior and came to Christ through a Baptist Church in the adjacent city of Duluth, Bob Dylan's hometown. A billboard on I-35 north of Minneapolis proclaims, "Next to Duluth, we are Superior."

Paul graduated with a Communications degree from the University of Minnesota at Duluth and felt God's call to ministry. He started a new church in Superior where he met Whitney, a summer missionary from Texas. They fell in love, and married.

When we met, Paul had been struggling for several years to get the church in Superior off the ground. They averaged about 50, sometimes surging to 80 and falling back to 50 or less. They were all young adults and young couples. When I joined them for prayer one evening I remarked it was the first church prayer session I had attended where no one requested prayer for a gall bladder or some other illness. They were focused on praying for their lost friends.

Nonetheless, the church was stuck as a close-knit single-cell congregation.

Perhaps from frustration or desperation Paul felt he should pursue a Seminary degree. We put together a scholarship and helped him enroll at Bethel Seminary in St. Paul, Minnesota. He knocked the top out. Years later he would receive the Outstanding Alumnus Award from Bethel. When he graduated he came to see me.

"God is calling us to start a church in Eau Claire, Wisconsin," he said. His earnest sincerity was obvious.

"If God has called you there," I said, "we will help you get there."

We put together some support so that Paul and Whitney could move to Eau Claire. He spent more than a year developing a core group and networking with existing churches in the area. In 2000 they launched Jacob's Well with 200 in attendance. Today Jacob's Well is located on highway 53 between Eau Claire and Chippewa, Wisconsin. They average more than 2,000.

...

I first met Mulenga Chella in August, 2013. When we moved to Waco, Texas the Lord impressed us to start a Bible study in our home for International students. Mulenga showed up at the first meeting, recently arrived from Zambia. He had been in the United States for only a few days. I asked him to tell me his story.

He had come to Christ in Ndola, Zambia's third largest city. God called him to preach as a teenager in Bread of Life Church in Ndola. He was encouraged to begin his journey in ministry immediately starting with his deep passion for the less privileged. His heart was drawn to the abandoned children on the streets of Ndola. For the next three years he reached out to these children sharing the gospel and providing meals one day a week.

When he was 20 he became pastor of a church of 16 people in Luanshya. It grew and flourished. From there God called him to a small church in the bush meeting in a mud hut with a thatched roof. Most in the village lived in similar mud thatched single-room homes. Those who were better off had shoes. The few members who came sat on mud bricks to listen to Mulenga preach. Overcoming spiritual forces of darkness, the church more than tripled.

Three times Mulenga heard prophetic words telling him he must endure prison in order to fulfill his calling to God. Ten months later he agreed to accompany an African missionary into Tanzania to help orphans, widows and the poor. After arriving in Tanzania, he discovered the "missionary" was a fraud and was arrested along with his companions and thrown into a Tanzanian prison. He remained in prison for 2 years, enduring inhumane conditions, learning to pray for his enemies.

After two years the man who deceived him was ill and dying. Against the counsel of the guards, Mulenga took care of him and nursed him back to health. He did so because Christ commanded him to love his enemies. That act of kindness eventually led to his release when the same man who first deceived him testified on his behalf and exonerated him. "If I had not loved my enemy, as Jesus commanded," Mulenga said, "I would still be in prison n in Tanzania." I helped edit

Mulenga's story *The Call To Surrender* which was published in 2015.

From the first day I met Mulenga, he had a vision of returning to Zambia to start a church and build a school. After completion of his Masters of Divinity degree he remained true to God's vision. He and Helen returned to Zambia and started Christ Life Church in Lusaka. The church "exists to support the transformation of the lives of our church members as well as prisoners, hospital patients, college students, children and people struggling with addiction."

All of these stories are, of course, anecdotal. But they reflect the timeless principle that is abundantly evident in the book of Acts and Christian history. Whenever men and women are captivated by a vision from God they are unstoppable. They can endure any setback, any discouragement. They will not be deterred. They endure and God uses them to change the world.

The list is long: Polycarp, Irenaeus, Augustine, Francis of Assissi, John Hus, William Tyndale, Martin Luther, John Calvin, John and Charles Wesley, George Whitfield, William Carey, Adoniram Judson, Charles Spurgeon, D. L. Moody, Billy Graham, Mother Theresa. None of these were flawless. But they were all driven by a vision from God that changed the world. For everyone listed there are a hundred more less known. And for each of them there are 10,000 more unknown and unrecognized that span every generation and every nation.

To be an effective church planter anywhere on the earth, first seek a vision from God.

Questions for discussion:

1. What difference did Paul's vision at Troas make in Paul's life, in the lives of his companions and in the history of Christianity?
2. Have you ever known someone who had a compelling vision from God?
3. Have you ever felt a compelling vision from God for your own life?
4. Describe what you believe is God's vision for your church.

CHAPTER FOUR

ETHNICITY

"Go therefore and make disciples of all the nations." (Matthew 28:19). In this statement, Jesus selected a precise word for the term, "nations." It is the word *ethne*, the root of the English term "ethnic." Why did He not say, make disciples of "all men" (*anthropoi*) or "all mankind" or "of the world" (*kosmos*)? Why did He choose *ethne*?

The Old Testament

Jesus' choice of this term is a fulfillment of God's expressed purpose. From the beginning, His plan to redeem humanity was couched in ethnic terms. God's call to Abraham to leave Haran and journey southward was a call with a purpose: "In you all the families of the earth shall be blessed." (Genesis 12:3).

The prophets recognized this truth and called Israel to respond to redemptive responsibilities beyond their borders. Micah prophesied, "And many nations shall come, and say, 'Come, and let us go up to the mountain of the Lord, and to the house of the God of Jacob; and He will teach us of His ways, and we will walk in His paths; for the law shall go forth of Zion, and the word of the Lord from Jerusalem."(Micah 4:2). Isaiah wrote, "Behold you will call a nation you do not know, and a nation that knows you not shall run to you, because of the Lord your God, even the Holy One of Israel; for He has glorified you." (Isaiah 55:5). Daniel said, "And to Him was given dominion, Glory and a kingdom, that all the peoples, nations and people of every language might serve Him." (Daniel 7:14). The Psalmist sang, "I will give thanks to you, O Lord, among the peoples; and I will sing praises unto you among the nations." (Psalm 57:9).

There are, of course, many more such references. This agreement between the prophets and the Great Commission is neither incidental nor accidental.

The Ministry of Jesus

God's desire to frame His redemptive strategy in terms of the nations is evident in the life of Jesus. He is constantly aware of the ethnic and cultural issues which shape perceptions of the kingdom message. He infuriated the citizens of Nazareth by reminding them that God sent Elijah to a Sidonian widow and Elisha to a leprous Syrian nobleman, while in Israel many widows and lepers suffered in poverty and disease. He astounded His disciples by not only traveling through the region of Samaria, but departing from His schedule to remain there two additional days to preach to those whom the Jews considered racially, culturally and spiritually inferior. He carefully refused to let the good news become identified with any one cultural expression when He replied to the Samaritan woman, "An hour is coming when neither in this mountain nor in Jerusalem will you worship the Father. ... true worshippers will worship the Father in spirit and truth." (John 4:21-23). He did not hesitate to plant the gospel in any culture, thereby allowing the regenerate life to find a variety of expressions. The Galileans, Judeans, Samaritans, Syro-Phonecians and Gadarenes would have hardly expressed their faith in identical ways. Their languages and dialects as well as regional and national traditions varied greatly.

Jesus' redemptive ministry recognized the ethnic structures of the world.

The Early Church

The book of Acts records the process by which the *Paraclete* continued to move the early church beyond ethnic boundaries of culture and language.

44

The Pentecost experience swaddled the newly born *ekklesia* in the multi-colored cloth of the *ethne*: "Partheans and Medes and Elamites and residents of Mesopotamia, Judea and Cappadocia, Pontus and Asia, Phrigia and Pamphylia, Egypt and the districts of Libya around Cyrene, and visitors from Rome, both Jews and proselytes, Cretans and Arabs – we hear them in our own tongues speaking of the mighty deeds of God." (Acts 2:9-11).

Even in this spiritually empowered beginning, the newly formed body of Christ had difficulty envisioning its existence outside a mono-cultural faith. From the moment of its birth, the church struggled with its task to make disciples of every culture, language and nation in the world. The Apostles did not conceive of "church" apart from Judaism. Yet they were soon faced with the possibility of new believers from outside these traditions.

Peter's Caesarean experience sent shock waves through the Christian community. So significant was his vision on the housetop in Joppa followed by the conversion of Cornelius, a Roman centurion, and his family, that this incident is recorded three times in Acts: first as it occurred (Acts 10), second as initially reported by Peter (Acts 11), and finally as "exhibit A" at the Jerusalem council (Acts 15).

This incident above all else moves the first century church to abandon circumcision as a requirement for Christian discipleship. The theological implications of this decision, that salvation should be by faith in Christ alone, has already been explored. But the practical implications of this decision, both for the first century and for today, are often overlooked. The rite of circumcision was the strongest expression of cultural identity among the Jews. It was the link with Abraham, Isaac and Jacob. But Peter's experience along with what Paul and Barnabas observed on their missionary expedition, forced the church to re-examine its stance. Would the Christian faith be disseminated only among groups which could identify with the Jewish culture and heritage, or would it be planted in all cultural contexts? The first century church chose the latter.

Paul's Preaching

Paul adapted his preaching to the cultural contexts in which he found himself. In synagogues he preached of the Exodus, the anointing of Saul, the greatness of David and the messianic prophecies of Christ. At Lystra he preached about the God of creation who called men from polytheistic worship to a living faith. At Athens he preached of the unknown god, creator of the cosmos and all humanity. He called all to repentance and faith. His preaching always centered on the redemptive resurrection of Christ. But his approach was determined by cultural perceptions.

In his letter to the Galatians, Paul clearly explained the theological implications of the Jerusalem Council decision regarding circumcision. He goes a step further by dropping the instruction to abstain from meat offered to idols. That this was a pointless issue in cultures outside Judaism surfaces in Paul's letter to the Romans (Romans 14). He establishes practical principles which foster respect for various cultural expressions of the Christian faith. Paul's "persuasion of the Lord" is a persuasion that refused to identify the Christian faith with any particular cultural expression. This conviction is set in bold relief against the pre-conversion convictions of Paul the "Pharisee of the Pharisees."

Today's Church and Ethnicity

The dilemma of the early church continues today. Like a rocket exerting thousands of pounds of thrust to break away from earth's gravitational pull, the church must make a concerted effort to free itself from the drag of cultural forces.

Unattended, the church is drawn into cultural orbit. It assumes its cultural values are identical with the Christian message.

The gospel does not require people of every race and socio-economic strata to worship in the manner of "our" church, to dress as "we" dress, think as "we" think, speak as "we" speak. The gospel of Jesus Christ must transcend culture to reach all people of every nation.

Every culture has its own language, food, music, dress and tradition. This is why Paul felt he must write Romans 14. These are not issues on which judgement should be made of one people opposed to another. Each church must choose its culture. Any church can be multi-ethnic, but few churches can be multi-cultural. Most congregations will choose the language, music, food and traditions determined by the context in which the church is planted and the people who make up the congregation. Few can celebrate various languages, foods and customs as a multi-cultural body.

I have visited six continents and 17 countries. I have worshipped with believers in various cultures. I have been inspired in every context. I find it exhilarating to see Jesus exalted in different languages with different music, to fellowship with believers around different foods. In each I have witnessed the radiant faces of joy and faith that transcends and permeates every culture. I have seen dim reflections of John's vision in Revelation:

"After these things I looked and behold a great multitude which no one could count, from every nation and all tribes and peoples and tongues, standing before the throne and before the Lamb, clothed in white robes and palm branches were in their hands; and they cry out with a loud voice saying, 'Salvation to our God who sits on the throne, and to the Lamb!'" (Revelation 7"9-10).

My good friend Stan Weese moved from Maryland to Minnesota thirty years ago to serve as pastor of North Center Baptist Church in Brooklyn Park. Stan grew up in West Virginia in a non-Christian home. His father was a professing atheist. But God wonderfully saved Stan and called him into the ministry. In Brookly Park, he found his church, over time, surrounded by a growing population of Liberian refugees who settled in the Twin Cities. 20,000 Liberians who fled civil war in Liberia live in Minnesota. Today two thirds of the North Center church are Liberian. In 2002 Stan led his church to help sponsor Ebeneezer Baptist Church in Brooklyn Park, a Liberian church led by Francis Tabla. A couple of years ago I attended the dedication of Ebeneezer Baptist Church with approximately 1,000 in attendance. Stan spoke. Both churches are continuing to reach Liberian people.

We are witnessing a rise in Xenophobia that I have not seen in my lifetime. It seems to me to be a ploy of the adversary who constantly seeks to sow suspicion, fear, prejudice and hate between individuals, peoples and nations. At the same time we are witnessing the greatest migration of people groups in the history of the world. Those who are believers need to ask themselves, "What is God doing in these migrations? How does he want to use this for His glory?" People who are desperately searching for safety, security and a new life are often open to the gospel.

In 1975, I was pastor of Franklin Baptist Church, a county-seat church in central Texas. Vietnamese refugees were pouring into the United States following the fall of South Vietnam. A settlement of these refugees sprang up nearby. We reached out to them and used our church bus to transport some to our church on Sundays. They sat in the back, listening, many of them unable to understand English. Some of our church members who harbored bitter feelings and deep wounds following the Vietnam War left the church.

Years later I met Frank Dang. Frank grew up in Vietnam. His father had been a medic in the South Vietnamese army. When the country fell his father was imprisoned and, when released, unable to gain employment. He escaped as one of the boat people, desperate to find a future. At sea the tiny boat began to sink. A missionary had urged Frank's father to call out to God and He would answer. In desperation, even though he was not a believer, he cried out like Peter sinking in the sea, "Lord, save me."

Out of the fog a ship appeared. He was rescued along with the others and taken to an island as a refugee where he heard the gospel and came to faith in Christ. After arriving in New Orleans, Frank's father joined a Vietnamese Baptist church and saved his money to bring his family to the United States. Sixteen years later Frank was able to join his father. By that time Frank had grown up as a Buddhist in Communist Vietnam, but through the witness of his father and friends he came to faith in Christ. Frank says, "I always knew Buddha was not God. But I did not know who God was."

Frank later graduated *summa cum laude* from Tulane University and entered the PhD program in math. But his heart was burdened for his people in Vietnam. He dropped out of the program, moved to Fort Worth, took a teaching position and entered Southwestern Seminary. In 2004 I asked Frank to join our staff to launch a mission organization for Texas Baptists. Today he is pastor of a Vietnamese church in Fort Worth and continuing to lead efforts to reach his people in Vietnam.

In 2013 we started an international Bible study in our home for grad students at Baylor University. The students came from China, Indonesia, South Africa, Vietnam, the Czech Republic, Zambia and the United States.

Hope grew up in rural China and never heard the name of Jesus until she went to university in Beijing. It was there she met a Christian missionary who told her about Jesus for the first time. She became involved in a house church, came to faith in Christ, earned a degree in English literature and became an interpreter for missionary groups visiting China. Hope invited a young visiting scholar from China, who was a leader among the young Communists. After several months, he came to faith in Christ and was baptized before returning to China.

They have all graduated and dispersed to the ends of the earth but they continue to encourage each other through social media. Christ, not culture, becomes the link, the common ground. In Him, children of differing cultures become "family."

These stories are only representative. They can be multiplied a million times over. Every day God is doing awesome things to fulfill His desires that all peoples of every language, tribe and nation come to know His saving grace in Jesus Christ. He has given us an incredible opportunity to join Him in a remarkable hinge of history to see His work fulfilled.

For too long the church has looked at the mission field around it and seen men "as trees walking." A second touch of the Great Physician's hand is needed that men may be seen clearly. (Mark 8:23-25).

Adjectives and Nouns

It is helpful to understand the differing cultural and racial distinctives as adjectives rather than nouns. An individual should be perceived as a unique person, neither an adjective nor a stereotype. The Laotian person is not merely, "Laotian." The Muslim person is not merely "Muslim." The non-professional worker should be seen as an individual and not merely "blue collar."

The Apostle's most definitive statement on this matter is found in Galatians: "There is neither Jew nor Greek, there is neither slave nor free man, there is neither male nor female; for you are all one in Christ Jesus" (Galatians 3:28). With this sweeping statement, the Scripture dissolves all distinctions in terms of worth and value. Subsequently all that is left is a "noun," a person. All are one in Christ Jesus regardless of racial or cultural identity. At the same time the Bible does not dismiss the distinctive uniqueness of racial and cultural groups preserving these as adjectives.

There are different characteristics between Jew and Gentile, male and female, bond and free. The Apostle recognizes these differences in his statement to the Corinthians: "To the Jews I became a Jew that I might win the Jews; to those who are under the Law as under the Law though not being myself under that Law, so that I might win those who are under the Law; to those who are without law, as without the law, though not being without the law of God but under the law of Christ, that I might win those who are without law; to the weak I became weak, that I might win the weak; I have become all things to all men that I may by all means win some" (1 Corinthians 9:20-22).

The Apostle recognized that the various cultural groups of his day would only be reached if the strategy for reaching them took into account these differences. The call of the gospel is a call to recognize the worth and dignity of all men, not a call to bury our heads in the sand and pretend no differences exist.

New Wine in Old Wineskins

It is helpful to understand the ethnic dimension of the church in terms of Jesus' parable of new wine in old wineskins. (Matthew 9:16-17). His reference to the inability of old and brittle wineskins to hold the swelling pressure of new wine is stimulated by his confrontation with the Jewish culture and traditions. His reference is clearly not to the law of God, for this law he embodied and fulfilled. Rather, he referred to a rigid culture that could not contain the power of the gospel.

Society is littered with the shards of shattered wine-skins. Every attempt to eliminate the cultural and traditional structures that separate races, nationalities and neighborhoods by force results in rage, revolt and deeper hostility. The semblance of unity may be maintained with the ability of the dominant culture to control education, language, economics and the media. But when "wineskins" break during open conflict, they reveal traditions and cultures that often harbor a multitude of sub-cultures.

The bursting of old wineskins is best done from within.

The unconverted Peter could hardly have envisioned himself in a Gentile home, let alone eating with Gentiles or defending their rights before his peers at Jerusalem. But the new wine of the gospel brought pressures from within that burst his earlier prejudices.

Perhaps even more dramatic is the story of Saul of Tarsus. This devoted Pharisee could scarcely conceive of a day when he would travel throughout the Gentile world promoting the inclusion of non-Jews into the messianic promise. But the brittle Pharisaic prejudices of his youth could not contain the wine of the new life in Christ.

More than thirty years ago I shared a meal with six Laotians, one Cambodian, one Native American and two Anglos in a Vietnamese restaurant. I have had many similar experience since. In 2012 I served as pastor of an English speaking church in Nuremberg, Germany, a small congregation composed mostly of young adults starting their careers in Nuremberg. They all spoke English as a first or second language. They came from India, South Africa, Cameroon, Ireland, the UK, Poland, Ukraine, Brazil, Germany and other nations. It was a fascinating and inspiring experience. The new wine of Christ had dissolved old wineskins that once separated their spiritual, intellectual and emotional lives. Even language difficulties become incidental under the love of Jesus Christ.

Church buildings once filled with scrubbed white faces and echoing English hymns of praise become home to people of many faces and many languages. Churches are discovering ways to share facilities among various ethnic groups, each with its distinctive cultural expression.

All discrimination and prejudice toward different groups should be unequivocally opposed by the Christian faith. Perhaps it is here that the world most flagrantly errs in its attempt to achieve racial equality. The dominant racial and cultural group assumes that others must become like *"us"* to possess equal worth and value.

To the world cultural differences pose a threat to stability and harmony. The Christian way affirms the worth and value of each person and defends, even promotes, the right to maintain cultural and racial differences. The focus must be on faith in Christ and obedience to His commands.

Churches in America too often make the assumption that conversion and Christian discipleship leads to expressions consistent with the Anglo culture. It is here that believers must divest themselves of one cultural identification and allow the gospel to find its expression in the various cultures in which it is planted.

The goal is not the eradication of meaningful adjectives that preserve differences of culture; the goal is the redemption of persons through the gospel of Jesus Christ.

The vast and rich personality of God demands that He be worshiped in a variety of languages and cultures. He is too great to be praised in one tongue, by one nation or one culture. If all peoples were integrated into one church, adopting one culture and one language, that would diminish the variety of praise of which He alone is worthy. (Revelation 5:11-13).

One final observation: while people will continue to group themselves around socio-economic, cultural and ethnic similarities, these conditions do not constitute the foundations of the church. They may describe expressions that the church will take in this diverse world, but they are not a foundation. There is no other foundation than that which is laid. "For no man can lay a foundation other than the one which is laid, which is Jesus Christ" (1 Corinthians 3:11).

The one foundation is Jesus Christ.

Questions for pastors and churches

1. Is our church open to receiving persons of all races?
2. Do we have members from various ethnic groups?
3. Are there different ethnic groups in our community?
4. Due to culture and language, would some people feel uncomfortable in our church?
5. Could our church sponsor congregations from various ethnic groups in our community?
6. Does our church have space it could make available to an ethnic congregation?
7. Is our church and its mission truly founded upon the person of Jesus Christ?

CHAPTER FIVE

NETWORKING

Networks refer to those connections by which people relate to people. Networks are the frequently traveled communication links that make life workable, meaningful and enjoyable. Networks are established along lines of common interest, mutual support and essential communication for performance of tasks. People build their networks through family, neighborhood, occupation and recreation.

In some cases, network development will relate closely to geography. In other cases, it will not. The simple geographic grouping of people does not necessarily identify the "networks" relating people to people.

If networks were imagined as connecting lines, they would vary in darkness or weight. Strong network lines, often within the immediate family, would appear heavy or dark. Network lines between employees and business associates might be medium weight, yet these, too, would be fairly distinct due to the common work hours and interdependence. Lighter, weaker lines would tie casual acquaintances and those persons encountered on an infrequent basis. Broken lines might characterize neglected relationships.

Networks in the New Testament

When Jesus launched His public ministry He used networks of relationship. I suppose Jesus had visited Capernaum many times during His youth. It was only a short distance from Nazareth. His first followers came from Capernaum and He made this lakeside village His base of operations.

Interestingly, Jesus' first connections appear to have taken place many miles away, in the location where John was baptizing on the Jordan, just north of the Dead Sea, southeast of Jerusalem. John's fame was so far flung that he attracted people from as far away as Galilee, including some fishermen from Capernaum. They had put aside their fishing and traveled several days, in search of the Messiah.

They likely had heard the reports that John had identified the Messiah. The heavens had opened and a voice had been heard. But, almost immediately, the one identified had disappeared. More than a month had passed -- plenty of time for the news to travel to Galilee, and plenty of time for the fishermen to make their way to John's baptismal site.

Andrew and John hung around after the preaching and the baptizing, close enough to see the fire in John's eyes when he saw Jesus. They heard John, perhaps speaking only to himself in a quiet voice filled with awe and wonder as he said, "Behold, the Lamb of God who takes away the sin of the world."

No one else seemed to recognize the man on whom John fixed his gaze. Otherwise Jesus surely would have been surrounded. John and Andrew did not hesitate. They immediately followed him. Jesus saw them first and asked them, "What are you looking for?" They stumbled, not knowing what to say. "Rabbi, where are you staying?" He must have smiled. "Come, and see."

We don't know how long they visited with Jesus that evening. We don't know what was said. We only know that by the time they left, they were convinced. They immediately found Simon, Andrew's brother and brought him to Jesus. "We have found the Messiah!" (John 1:41). The networking had begun.

With this experience in the background, it is no wonder that all three of them, along with James, left their nets and followed

Jesus when he saw them again at the sea of Galilee. They were joined by Philip who also found Nathanael (John 1:43-51). The networking within the initial gathering of the 12 is unmistakable.

Jesus would later build upon this principle when he taught his followers how to reach entire villages with the Kingdom message. He introduced them to the *oikos* principle. *Oikos* is the Greek word that literally means "house." It is often translated "household." It appears that it was often used for the close-knit sphere of influence that every person has.

When Jesus sent out the 70 in Luke 10, he specifically instructed them to use this principle to penetrate the towns and villages where he sent them. "Whatever house you enter, first say, 'Peace be to this house.' If a man of peace is there, your peace will rest on him; but if not, it will return to you. Stay in that house, eating and drinking whatever they give you. ... Do not keep moving from house to house" (Luke 10:5-7).

Every time the word "house" appears in this passage, it is the Greek word *oikos*. It is more than a physical structure for shelter. *Oikos* represents the networks of relationship that this "person of peace" has within that village. By staying with the person whose heart is already warm and open to the Gospel, they were able to penetrate the networks of relationship throughout that community. By applying this principle, 70 disciples returned from their assignment saying, "Lord, even the demons are subject to us in your name!" (Luke 10:17). This is the principle that is being applied in every region where church planting movements are taking place.

Paul learned this networking principle through practical experience. When he and Barnabas started their first journey, they missed the opportunity in Cyprus. God did some amazing things on Cyprus and the proconsul Sergius Paulus came to faith. But this word *oikos* is strangely missing. It appears they did not follow up with the relationships that Sergius Paulus would have surely had on the island.

After they successfully took the time to plant churches in Antioch of Pisidia, Lystra, Iconium and Derbe, they apparently realized the importance of the *oikos* principle.

On Paul's second journey, they began looking for *oikos* relationships. When they reached Philippi they spent some days trying to decide where to start, a common experience for most church planters. There was no synagogue, so, they wandered out to the riverside where they "supposed there would be a place of prayer" (Acts 16:13). We don't know how many people were gathered at the riverside, but one stood out, a woman named Lydia. She was warm and responsive, a "person of peace." So they spent their time with her and, when she responded with faith to their message about Christ, they focused on her *oikos*.

Specifically, Luke took note that Lydia had recently arrived in Philippi from Thyatira. She was a businesswoman, a seller of purple fabrics. Who her family was, we don't know. But when Lydia came to faith in Christ, those who were part of her *oikos* did too. "And when she and her household had been baptized, she urged us, saying, 'If you judged me to be faithful to the Lord, come into my house and stay.'" (Acts 16:15). Surely counted among her *oikos* were her family members along with business associates, suppliers, buyers and vendors for purple fabrics. Perhaps there were others from Thyatira. We don't know for sure. The nucleus of a church was born.

It wasn't long before, in the same city, Paul and Silas found themselves falsely accused and thrown into prison. With their feet in stocks, imprisoned in a dark and damp cell that reeked of sweat, they sang hymns of praise. These were strange sounds to the Roman jailer's ears who was accustomed to the curses and complaints of the prisoners.

An earthquake struck during the night. The ground shook so violently that the doors were ripped from their hinges and the stocks were splintered. Assuming the prisoners had escaped, the prison guard unsheathed his sword and prepared to take his own life. He had likely come to this assignment by previous failures and this moment left him hopeless, on the brink of suicide. But from the shadows came a cry, "Do not harm yourself, for we are all here!" (Acts 16:28).

It was Paul's voice. The prison guard was stunned. He took a lamp to examine the cell. Overwhelmed by the compassion, kindness and faith of these men, he fell to the ground, trembling, asking "Sirs, what must I do to be saved?" "Believe on the Lord Jesus," Paul answered "and you will be saved. You and your *oikos*" (Acts 16:22-31). Here is that word again! *Oikos*! Paul immediately saw the implications. If this man came to faith, others in his sphere of faith would come.

And they did: "And he took them that very hour of the night and washed their wounds, and immediately he was baptized, he and all his household. And he brought them into his house and set food before them, and rejoiced greatly, having believed in God with his whole *oikos*" (Acts 16:33-34).

We have all seen this many times over. When one person comes to faith in Christ, those in their immediate sphere of influence come to Christ.[20]

When Paul arrived at Corinth he struggled. It appears that he was discouraged and almost gave up. I know this sounds

---

[20] W. When I was in the doctor of ministry program at Southwestern on of my classmates was Oscar Thompson. Oscar wrote a book about this principle. Oscar Thompson, Concentric Circles of Concern. Oscar died in 1980. The book was updated and republished in 1999 by Carolyn Thompson Ritzman and Claude V. King.

incomprehensible for someone like Paul. But why else would God speak to him through a vision in the night? "Do not be afraid any longer, but go on speaking and do not be silent" (Acts 18:9). Over the years I have learned that discouragement is the church planter's greatest enemy. Even when there are obvious signs of success, church planters can become discouraged. Discouragement is seldom logical.

Paul met Priscilla and Aquila who would later become influential leaders in the first century movement. But at this time, this young couple had no influence in Corinth. Luke takes care to explain that Priscilla and Aquila had recently arrived from Rome. They were new residents in Corinth and had no *oikos* in the city.

Often church planters will seek out new residents. They are usually more open to making new commitments and forming new relationships. But they are often like Priscilla and Aquila. They have no influence with their neighbors.

The church in Corinth did not take off until Crispus, the leader of the synagogue came to faith in Christ. "Crispus, the leader of the synagogue believed with all his household, and many of the Corinthians when they heard were believing and being baptized" (Acts 18:8). Crispus had a significant *oikos* (household). When many of the Corinthians heard that Crispus had become a believer, they also believed. Networks of relationship are the most powerful force in reaching people with the gospel.

Networking in the 21st Century

Prior to the industrial and technological revolutions, the networks among people were much more closely defined. In rural, pre-industrial America, the networking among people was strong, easily identified and understood. Virtually all communication was carried out face-to-face.

Those days are past. Networking is now more complex. This has important implications for church strategies that address the Great Commission. Every community develops its unique system of networking. It is impossible to approach the concept of community networking with a simplistic design for every situation. However, communities have certain networking characteristics in common.

The suburban community

The advent of metroplex communities with commuter transportation and instant worldwide cell phone and internet communication has revolutionized the network dynamic. People who live next to one another in densely grouped apartments, condos and neighborhoods often do not know one another. Their networks are often job related and can exist a great distance from their suburban communities. They spend the best part of the day in constant communication with co-workers who may live an hour's drive in the opposite direction. Husbands and wives, or live-in significant others, commute in different directions, their work-day stretching from 6 a.m. to 6 p.m. or longer. When they return home they tend to hibernate in apartments, condominiums and houses. They feel alone in the midst of multitudes without neighborhood networks.

Suburban shopping reinforces the feeling of anonymity. Repeated trips to the grocery store remain encounters with unnamed people and unfamiliar faces. In shopping centers – hubs of great metropolitan regions – regular visits produce few networking relationships. The typical suburban dweller neither knows, nor is known by those who live around them.

Schools tend to remain the most powerful local networking systems still intact. Young families network around the educational and recreational activities of their children.

Neighborhood networks may be virtually non-existent, yet people do not live in a vacuum. Their network has simply expanded to a global community. Commuters spend the day with distant commuters. Sales people, corporate executives, graphic designers, IT experts, marketing specialists (the list is endless) often communicate daily with colleagues in Seattle, Dallas, Chicago, New York, Minneapolis, Mumbai, Cape Town, Jakarta, London, Paris, Berlin, Dubai, Mexico City, Guadalajara, Rio de Janeiro or Buenos Aires (to name a few). We live in a global village. Many have closer relationships with those on the other side of the continent or other countries than with those who live across the street.

The church planted in a pre-industrial, pre-technological age found ready root in fertile soil within local community networks. But the church planted in today's suburban fringe can find the soil stony and resistant. Many interpret as spiritual indifference what might be sociological realities. Network relationships have stretched beyond, and have formed outside the traditional community. In this context the church must provide networks for people who are starved to know and be known by those who live closest to them.

The rural community

Networking in the rural community is more similar to networking in the past. If the community is small enough, virtually everyone is known by name. One young woman who moved from a metropolitan home to a small town reported that her child returned from a neighborhood store reporting with disbelief, "Mom, they knew my name!"

Often networks in these communities have been reinforced for generations. While this produces strongly defined network lines within the community, the network can also become inflexible or closed. Newcomers, quickly known by face and name (which may appear to be acceptance) soon discover admittance is gained the "old fashioned way." They must earn it. This might not be accomplished in less than a generation. It is possible for a longtime resident to live perpetually outside the networks of "real" residents who were born there.

In these communities new residents are more easily reached by new churches with new networking opportunities.

The inner city

Metropolitan regions grow outward from the center, like growth rings on a tree. As a city grows it must develop transportation "loops" for commerce. In Dallas, it was first loop 12, then 635 followed by the George Bush Turnpike. In Chicago, it is Interstates 90, 294 and 355. In Minneapolis, it is I-94, MN 62 & 100, I 494 and 694. These major transportation loops become distinguishable barriers between the heaving inner city and its suburban sprawl.

From the reflective high rise office buildings to the bustling economy springing up along the loop, the city is traversed by thousands of commuters who never see the inner city. The inner city's mosaic of people is unknown, misunderstood and often distrusted.

The inner city is not a community. It is a composite of many communities, each formed by various socio-economic and ethnic dimensions. It contains distinct communities of people: Black, Hispanic, Chinese, Korean, Laotian, Vietnamese, Anglo and others. Alongside these ethnic communities are Anglos who have owned their homes for decades and have watched their neighborhoods inundated by change. Some are like Walt Kowalski (played by Clint Eastwood) in the movie, *Gran Torino.*

In 2010 Philadelphia was ranked 9th among the most segregated cities in America. 75% of the population in many neighborhoods were made up of a single racial group. After

2000 some of these areas began to be impacted by gentrification and the redevelopment of the city center.

A drive through the city reveals its contrast and variety. Signs, advertisements, shops, restaurants and housing change as if a page were turned in a book. From block to block, from complex to complex, distinguishable communities exist side by side. Within these communities people develop their indigenous networks.

A single apartment complex may house 2,000 to 3,000 people, larger than many small towns. These communities need churches for their unique socio-economic and ethnic populations.

Networking and the church

Churches often view their "field" in geographic terms, often drawing a two-mile radius to determine their area of responsibility, their turf. When residents within that circle are visited by "outside" churches it may be viewed as intrusion. But people do not necessarily attend churches within geographic boundaries. When "Sam Jones" trusts Christ as Savior and joins Trinity Church, he invites others to visit his newfound Christian family. He may have an aunt, uncle or cousin living in a distant neighborhood. They are apt to attend church with Sam and find faith where Sam found it. The same thing will be true concerning those who work with Sam. As a result, persons living in the shadow of First Church may drive several miles to attend Trinity Church, while others drive past Trinity to attend First Church.

Church members may be dismayed to discover they do not reach the people who live close to the church building. The church should consider this in the context of network dynamics. A church will most likely reach people through established network patterns. A church building may be surrounded by people who need a new church.

Responses to questionnaires (completed by people who attend church) indicated that family and friends are the strongest influence on where a person attends church. Very few indicated the influence of visits from a pastor; less influential were special events, buildings and programs. These factors are important to the life of a church, but are not perceived as the deciding factors for church attendance. Churches are made alive and effective by the living networks of people.

Churches grow along lines of communication and influence inherent in relationships among people. Lines of church growth are demographic rather than geographic. Churches will be more effective if they discover where the networks of their people exist and capitalize on these to reach others for Christ.

Because churches grow along network lines, churches can exist in close proximity to each other and yet reach an entirely different group of people. Churches need to be planted according to the unreached networks of people which exist in a community rather than by the location of pins on a map.

Networking and church growth

Understanding networking enables the church to channel its energies more effectively into areas that will reach more people. A church that recognizes that people are reached along lines of personal influence can begin using its best means for reaching others. A church with members who enjoy many networks within the community is a church that has great potential for growth.

Most churches become root bound. The members of the church spend most of their discretionary time networking with others who are within the church. Even their recreational activities for sports and social events are scheduled by the church and spent in connection with other church members. Instead of pulling people out of recreational and social community organizations, churches should treasure opportunities to participate in these groups where they will form friendships with non-believers and the unchurched.

Churches stop growing because the network potential within the congregation becomes saturated. People only have so much time to invest in forming and maintaining relationships. When visitors attend there is no time and energy remaining to form new friendships with them. All the internal networks are filled. To overcome this, churches must constantly look for ways to foster new small groups and plant new churches.

Networking and new churches

Communities that afford opportunities for creation and maintenance of new networks are fertile for new churches. This would be true of rapidly growing single family neighborhoods that are isolated from surrounding suburban and metropolitan communities. Such communities may be populated by many new residents anxious to establish new relationships with new neighbors. The public school system, the emerging recreation organizations, volunteer service groups and developing city government could provide rapidly expanding networks through which people interact.

Inner-city communities also can provide remarkably fertile soil for planting churches. Many inner-city communities are composed of distinct ethnic and cultural groups that have developed strong networks. Seeing themselves as a minority culture, be it Laotian, Cambodian, Hmong, Vietnamese, Black or Hispanic, they often develop an interdependent network for survival. Drawn together by language and culture, these communities often include large families with many relationships. Once the gospel has penetrated the network, it often spreads rapidly.

Rural communities may also offer fertile soil. Within these communities older established churches have often become "root bound" with internal networks that are unable to assimilate new members. Patriarchs of the community maintain decision-making positions within the church. New residents have difficulty finding a place.

Within these communities, there may exist an entire population that is beyond the reach of the established congregations. These could be reached and discipled by a new church. New churches offer open internal networks that can rapidly assimilate new members. A young congregation is eager to accept new members into the life of the church, to offer opportunities for service, leadership and friendship.

New churches retain a higher percentage of new members than do established older congregations. The older church may receive as many or even more new members, but will likely lose these within a relatively short time.

Total penetration with the gospel of Christ will not occur through churches that reach a reasonable percentage of a large geographic area but by churches that can penetrate every networking dimension of the world.

Churches may be needed in penthouses with multi-million dollar condominiums, in mobile home parks, apartment complexes, government subsidized housing units, as well as suburban communities and rural villages.

Two of the most successful churches in this effort have been First Baptist, Arlington, Texas with Mission Arlington under Tillie Bergin and Mosaic Church in Los Angeles, formerly the

Church on Brady led by Thom Wolf who launched the "oikos evangelism" model. Irwin McManus has led Mosaic since 1994.

The Apostle Paul became a master of networking relationships. His conclusion to the book of Romans is eye opening on this point. He goes to great lengths to list the key persons then in Rome who formed the networks whereby Rome was being discipled.

"Greet Priscilla and Aquila, my fellow workers in Christ Jesus, who for my life risked their own necks, to whom not only do I give thanks but also all of the churches of the Gentiles; also greet the church that is in their house. Greet Epaenetus, my beloved, who is the first convert to Christ from Asia. Greet Mary, who has worked hard for you. Greet Andronicus and Junias, my kinsmen and my fellow prisoners, who are outstanding among the apostles, who also were in Christ before me. Greet Ampliatus, my beloved in the Lord. Greet Urbanus, our fellow worker in Christ, and Stachys my beloved. Greet Apelles, the approved in Christ. Greet those who are of the *household* of Aristobulus. Greet Herodion, my kinsman. Greet those of the *household* of Narcissus, who are in the Lord. Greet Tryphaena and Tryphosa, workers in the Lord. Greet Persis the beloved, who has worked hard in the Lord. Greet Rufus, a choice man in the Lord, also his mother and mine. Greet Asyncritus, Phlegon, Hermes, Patrobas, Hermas and the brethren with them. Greet Philologus and Julia, Nereus and his sister, and Olympas, and all the saints who are with them. Greet one another with a holy kiss. All the churches of Christ greet you" (Romans 16:3-16).

Such lists of names in the Scripture are often glossed over as meaningless. But the message within this "incidental" record is critical. Here are the persons who formed the networks that unlocked Rome! The abundance of Greek and Roman names is obvious.

It should be noted that Priscilla and Aquila, who in Acts 18 had recently arrived in Corinth from Rome, had at this time, traveled full circle and returned to the Roman capital. They must have maintained many friends and acquaintances who became natural channels for the spread of the gospel in Rome. The New International Commentary on Romans cites J.B. Lightfoot's contention that Apelles of verse 10 "was a grandson of Herod the Great and of Agrippa and of Herod (King of Calcis) and on intimate relations with the Emperor Claudius." An elaborate and natural network of relationships must have existed throughout the city as these made disciples among their households and friends.

Conclusion

The church has always grown, and will continue to grow, along the lines of network relationships. Whenever an attempt is made to grow in any other way, growth becomes artificial and inevitably meets with defeat. If the church wants to succeed in fulfilling the Great Commision, it must discover the means of penetrating the existing networks of human relationships and plant congregations within the framework of each. It must discover the dynamics of networking within the local congregation and capitalize on these principles.

Questions for discussion:

1. What are the networks within our community?
2. What networks do the members of our church have within the community?
3. How could the gospel be communicated by the members of our church through their existing networks?
4. How could our church develop better networks in the community?
5. Could our church plant new churches within particular networks within our community?

6. What are the networks within our congregation?
7. Are these networks saturated?
8. How could our church be structured so that its networks are more open to assimilate new people?

CHAPTER SIX

INDIGENEITY

For a new church to succeed, it must become indigenous, growing naturally within its context. Otherwise it will remain a dependent ministry of another church, able to provide a valuable service, perhaps, but unable to take root and multiply. More than any other aspect of church planting, the indigenous dimension determines success or failure.

What is Indigenous?

Norman Wallace, a good friend and a master gardener, once gave what I thought was the best definition of "indigenous." He simply said that when something is indigenous, it "wants to grow there." This is certainly true of plants. It is also true of people and churches.

Over the years we have lived in Texas, Minnesota and Colorado. Each place has its own beauty and its own vegetation. They even smell different. In Texas we enjoyed the native pecans and live oaks. In Minnesota we had a blue spruce in our yard. In Colorado, where we now make our home, I enjoy morning meditations under an aspen tree out back. Each of these grow where "they want to grow." They are in the right place, with the right soil and the right climate to thrive.

Churches are like that too. When the people who make up a church are indigenous to that region, they take root, grow and bear fruit. They propagate and multiply just like the pecan in Texas, the spruce in Minnesota and the aspen in Colorado.

The Early Church

The successful mission enterprise of the first century was marked by indigenous leaders and resources. When the church at Antioch sent Saul and Barnabas on their first missionary journey, they had no intention to transfer Antiochian Christians to Cyprus, Iconium, Lystra, Philippi, Thessalonica and Corinth. Nor did they plan to finance the churches that would be started. Each mission effort would be indigenous in terms of leaders and resources.

As Paul, Barnabas and John Mark viewed Mount Olympus on the island of Cyprus rising above the sparkling Mediterranean, they must have wondered how this first mission effort would unfold. They must have seen the large commercial harbor at Salamis and its populated shores as an opportunity and obstacle. It was not until they made their way through the length of the island that they recorded their first success.

Sergius Paulus, proconsul on the island of Cypus, "a man of intelligence" (Acts 13:7), came to faith in Jesus Christ. An inscription dated AD 52-53 uncovered at the city of Paphos bears the words, "in the time of proconsul Paulus." This man, otherwise a mere name on an ancient inscription, became the first convert of the first mission journey.

The churches planted in the New Testament were indigenous churches. They did not import leadership from Jerusalem. Those who became pastors and elders were raised up from within the local body of those who came to faith in Christ. Immediately after planting the churches on their first missionary journey, Paul and Barnabas "returned to Lystra and to Iconium, and to Antioch of Pisidia strengthening the disciples and encouraging them to continue in the faith … When they appointed elders for them in every church, having prayed with fasting, they commended them to the Lord in whom they had believed" (Acts 14:21-23). Paul later wrote to his young protégé, Titus, "For this reason I left you in Crete, that you would set in order what remains and appoint elders in every city as I directed you" (Titus 1:5).

By raising up indigenous leadership from within, the young churches took root in their communities and grew, then reached out to other regions. To the Thessalonians, Paul wrote, "you became an example to all the believers in Macedonia and Achaia. For the word of the Lord has sounded forth from you, not only in Macedonia and Achaia, but in every place your faith toward God has gone forth" (1 Thessalonians 1:7-8).

Personal Lessons in Indigeneity

My wife and I are native Texans. My wife grew up in Freeport near Galveston. She did not see snow until she was a teenager. In 1993 the Lord called us to Minnesota and Wisconsin where I served as executive director for the Minnesota-Wisconsin Baptist Convention. In February I loaded my stuff into a 1989 Mitsubishi Galant, including my desk, and headed north while she stayed behind in Texas to finish the school year. The further I drove the colder it got. By the time I reached Iowa I was surrounded by snow-covered hills, frozen lakes and barns with silos. Nothing looked familiar. I wasn't even sure I could survive. I started asking myself, "What have I done?"

It was a steep cultural learning curve.

I soon discovered that I was not alone. There were many Southern transplants who had moved to Minnesota and Wisconsin over the past few decades. They had found each other and formed Southern Baptist churches that were part of the Minnesota-Wisconsin Southern Baptist Convention. In many cases, they maintained all they loved about being from the South. They talked about the South; they rooted for their Southern alma-maters; they ate southern foods together and they played forty-two, a domino game native to Texas. They spoke with a Southern twang. When they needed a new pastor, they looked to the South and moved someone in.

Don't get me wrong. I love Southerners. I love Texas. I love my family roots. But it was clear to me that our churches were "out of place." We were not indigenous to the upper Midwest. The Southerners who formed these churches never fully assimilated into their new environment. But their children adapted. They grew up with friends in Minnesota-Wisconsin, learned to speak with an upper Midwestern accent when they wanted, thought nothing of going out in sub-zero weather, loved skiing, snow mobiling, ice fishing, ate lefse and some even tried lutefisk. When they left home they joined non-Southern Baptist churches where their friends went.

Perhaps it is needless to say that these churches were not growing. They had grown quickly when they first started scooping up Southern transplants in the 1950s and 60s. But by the 1990s they were plateaued or declining, and they were not reproducing. Why? They were not indigenous.

I was aware of the indigenous principle. After all, I included a chapter on indigeneity in this book when it was first published in 1986. But now I was experiencing the indigenous principle up close and personal. I needed help.

I turned to Lyle Schaller. Christianity Today called Lyle "the dean of church consultants." He had written 55 books and was named the most influential Protestant leader in 1988-1989. Lyle grew up on a dairy in Wisconsin and started his ministry in Wisconsin. When I called him he said he could come to Rochester, Minnesota and spend the day. It would cost at least $1,000. Or, I could come to Chicago and we could have lunch. I drove to Chicago and we had lunch.

Of all the things Lyle told me that day, two things stuck. First, he suggested I meet Leith Anderson, pastor of Woodway

Church in Eden Prairie, Minnesota. Second, that I consider making Bethel Seminary our seminary. I had read Leith Anderson's book, *Dying for Change* and I was anxious to meet him. I had never heard of Bethel Seminary, but I would check them out.

Leith agreed to meet me for lunch based on an introduction by Lyle Shaller. His first comment was, "I don't think Southern Baptists can succeed up here." With that beginning, we formed a strong friendship and a few years later worked together to start a new church in Maple Grove, Minnesota. I invited him several times to speak to our pastors. He graciously accepted and was warmly received.

I discovered Bethel Seminary was operated by the Baptist General Conference, which later changed its name to Converge. We created a scholarship that would provide a Southern Baptist track at Bethel in order to retain emerging leadership in Minnesota and Wisconsin rather than losing them to SBC seminaries more than 500 miles away. (Distance learning options were not yet available. The internet was in its infancy). Paul Berthiaume, pastor of Jacobs Well in Eau Claire, Wisconsin was one of our first graduates. Paul grew up in Superior, Wisconsin. His story is include in the chapter on vision.

We reconsidered our name, Minnesota-Wisconsin Southern Baptist Convention. On a recommendation from Gerald Palmer, retired vice president of the SBC Home Mission Board and a native Wisconsite, we dropped "Southern." We began to change our identity from "Southern Baptists working in Minnesota-Wisconsin" to "Minnesota-Wisconsin Baptists who cooperate with the Southern Baptist Convention."

We launched "Empower" conferences to "empower the laity," focusing on indigenous leadership.

Leo Endel, who was a successful pastor in Iowa, followed me as Executive Director for MWBC in 2002. He moved all of these initiatives forward and built on them. Today the churches are far more indigenous. New churches are being started every month. Leo and I have become devoted friends. At his request, I continue to lead pastor peer learning groups in Minnesota and Wisconsin.

Ownership, Leadership and Resources

Jeff Christopherson expressed this principle best in his book, *Kingdom First*: "Perhaps one of the biggest reasons as to why a new church does not gain sufficient traction in a given community is because locals see it as a grand company of interlopers and outsiders. Great care and attention should be given to developing and highlighting leaders who are already indigenous to their community. The only church planting path that is sustainable in the long term is the way of developing a local leadership base. Any shortcut to that goal usually yields an anemic and sterile assembly with little reproductive viability." [21]

The indigenous principle complements the ethnic dimension, yet it is broader in application. Human beings are indigenous to particular regions and cultural climates. When people from a distinct sociological/ethnic group migrate to a new region, they take with them their culture. They thrive within their context of language, religion, food, dress and art. Each ethnic group contains cultural sub-groups reflecting further distinctions.

Often the gospel fails to penetrate a particular group because the message is identified with cultural values rather than the Christian faith. For instance, the Western wedding ceremony is not taken from Scripture. The Bible is silent concerning this and other ceremonies related to birth, death and worship.

---

[21] Jeff Christopherson, *Kingdom First* (Nashville, TN. B&H Publishing Group,2015) Kindle edition, 3027.

According to the indigenous principle, the gospel may find a variety of cultural expressions without compromising the message of the crucified and resurrected Christ. These meaningful life passages may be celebrated and observed in different ways in many cultures. Only as the body of Christ expands to include all cultures of this complex world will the strategy of Jesus be fulfilled.

If a new church is to succeed, all aspects of ownership must shift from the sponsoring group into the hands of those who comprise the new congregation. This issue must be handled with sensitivity, particularly in the areas of leadership and resources. Without leaders from "among the people" the new church will struggle and perhaps die. A new church largely funded by outside sources for an extended time will become a disabled limb in the body of Christ.

Indigenous church planting purists exclude any outside leadership or financial support from the very beginning. Others allow limited outside leadership and assistance to be used like kindling recognizing the danger that once the "kindling" has been consumed there is no guarantee that the indigenous logs will ignite. The fire and flame must be transferred to indigenous leadership.

China serves as a case in point regarding the power of indigeneity. In 1860 there were 50 Western missionaries in China, which grew to 2,500 by 1900. But in 1953 there were none. They had been expelled by the Communist revolution under Mao Zedong . Many of these missionaries lived out inspiring and courageous stories of faith. Their names have lived on as heroes of the faith, among them: Lottie Moon, Bill Wallace, C. T. Studd and Eric Liddell. Their work bore fruit. The number of Christians in China grew from 100,000 in 1900 to 700,000 in 1950.

With the removal of all outside influence and support, the indigenous believers who were left in China were forced to become leaders. They created house churches that reproduced with leaders raised up from within despite continued persecution. The churches in China multiplied. The number of Christians grew from less than 1 million in 1950 to 67 million in 2018, less than 70 years after missionaries were expelled.

David Garrison explained the importance of the indigenous principle in church planting movements that he studied. "Indigenous literally means *generated from within*, as opposed to started by outsiders. In Church Planting Movements the first church or churches may be started by outsiders, but very quickly the momentum shifts from the outsiders to the insiders. Consequently, within a short time, the new believers coming to Christ in Church Planting Movements may not even know that a foreigner was ever involved in the work. In their eyes the movement looks, acts, and feels homegrown." [22]

The courageous early missionaries who gave their lives in China started something. When they were expelled through Communism, the Chinese believers who remained under persecution created something entirely indigenous. The movement exploded and continues.

Ironically the greatest obstacle to indigenous church planting movements in the United States is the legacy of Western Christendom. When we attempted to initiate a Church Planting Movement in Minnesota and Wisconsin in the 1990s by empowering the laity to plant churches in "every city and place," we discovered that the Christendom culture was so deeply engrained that it could not gain traction. No sooner did a house church form than they began looking for a paid pastor

---

[22] David Garrison, *op. cit.,* Kindle edition 263.

and seeking a building. They quickly fell into the Christendom mold.

This could change. The United States is becoming increasingly secular and we are moving further into a post-Christendom world. As we do so, we may see greater potential for an indigenous Church Planting Movement. Until then, we will have to start churches as quickly as possible using the best church planting methods available to us.

Practical applications of indigeneity and church planting

Many older churches are reluctant to start a new church that is similar to their own. They are afraid they must send out a large number of their members to start this new congregation. At the same time, would-be church planters are afraid to start a new church without a substantial nucleus of people from the sponsor church.

But, according to the indigenous principle, a new church will start and grow more effectively with the help of only a few sponsoring members who are compatible with those living in the target area.

Occasionally a new church is launched with a large number of members drawn from the sponsoring church. If these persons are already closely related to each other, and especially if they do not live in the target area, the new church may soon find itself in the throes of a spiritual abortion.

For example, more than once I have seen new churches launched with a significant number of members from the sponsor church. In one case the target area was near the sponsoring church. Both were middle to upper-middle class Anglo communities. But the target area was composed of mostly young, upwardly mobile adults in a developing neighborhood with new houses and new streets. The sponsoring group was older. They sent 35 older adults to start the new church, most of them driving into the new neighborhood. On their first Sunday, 45 attended. A year later they were averaging 30. The new church was struggling and questioning its future. It will probably not grow until some of the younger adults living in the new neighborhood assume ownership and leadership of the new church. In many cases, that does not happen.

When a significant number of mature Christian adults are enlisted to start a new church the ability of the new church to reach the lost and unchurched is reduced. Those with a non-Christian background are confused by the accepted religious terms and concepts. Pre-Christian and new Christian attenders need groups with basic discussions about faith in language that is free of religious jargon.

When we started a church in 1976 we attracted a number of young electrical engineers. They were on the cusp of the technological revolution that changed our world. I struggled with their professional jargon and toured manufacturing plants to learn more about hardware, software, and micro-chips. The Apple PC wasn't invented by Steve Jobs and Steve Wozniak until 1977. IBM followed with its first PC in 1981. Terms that are now common and permeate our English (and non-English) language were just being introduced. Many did not exist. It was a whole new vocabulary.

The lost and unchurched face a similar challenge that I faced when they are thrown into a group that commonly refer to "pre-mellinial," the "Parousia," "Judaizers," Saul, Paul and three different people named John along with a guy named Simon who is also called Peter. Those who are part of the church culture assume Old Testament, New Testament, the Gospels, and the letters of Paul. And they know where and how to find them. Besides, today few have seen a Bible. Most look up Scripture on cell phones and e-readers. Long term church members make numerous assumptions about Christian terms, concepts and references.

A church structured with new converts in positions of leadership may be less stable, yet these people will likely attract others from the world more quickly and easily. New churches serve best when they focus on the lost, un-enlisted and uninvolved.

Each church must be allowed to adopt the cultural expressions of its people; ownership must be sensitively nurtured; new churches must provide leadership opportunities for new converts and the previously unchurched while giving support and supervision. Resources must come from the people who are being reached.

Questions for discussion:

1. What does it mean for something to be indigenous?
2. Is our church indigenous to the community we are seeking to reach?
3. What are the indigenous cultural expressions of our church?
4. Do our people feel a sense of ownership in the church?
5. Does our church sponsor a new church?
6. If so, are we allowing the new church to be indigenous to its community?

CHAPTER SEVEN

THE HARVEST

We live in an age of religious affluence. Many churches have million dollar budgets. Denominations and religious organizations own and operate entire communications networks and publishing houses. Billions of dollars are donated to religious causes. The resources of the modern church are great. Yet in face of the need, the resources seem inadequate. Only one resource is inexhaustible in terms of reaching a lost world. And that is the harvest.

Resources in the Harvest

Jesus made a pivotal statement when He sat with His disciples at Jacob's well in Samaria near the village of Sychar. The Twelve had just returned from the nearby village where they purchased bread for their journey. When they returned they found Him deep in conversation with a Samaritan woman. They were shocked, not only that he was speaking with a woman, but that he was conversing with a Samaritan. If they had known her moral character, which Jesus knew, they would have been even more disturbed. What he said would revolutionize their thinking in future days. Jesus said, "Lift up your eyes and look on the fields; for they are white already for harvest" (John 4:35).

Jesus was speaking of people. Some think that he was referring to the crowds of Samaritans who were cresting the hill. Perhaps a period of time had elapsed after the woman returned to the village before Jesus made this dramatic statement. Possibly the men of Sychar were already coming to investigate the woman's report, If so, it would create a dramatic backdrop for Jesus' statement.

John tells us that many of the Samaritans believed because of the woman's testimony. After they invited Him to stay, Jesus remained two additional days visiting with the Samaritans. No wonder the first great awakening following Jesus' resurrection broke out in Samaria!

When Jesus spoke of the fields being "white for harvest," He not only identified the harvest as the urgent need – he also identified the harvest as the great resource.

Jesus could have said, "Look on the fields *for they are fertile for sowing.*" That would have required that the seed be provided by the sowers. This would have robbed the statement of its full implication. A field ripe for harvest is full of the seeds that will produce future crops. The image is powerful as the church of the 21st century fulfills its place in the harvest strategy of God.

Jesus' assignment to the 70 in Luke 10 is an object lesson in the harvest principle. As He sent the fearful disciples into every village and city, he specifically instructed them regarding resources. "Carry no purse, no bag, no shoes … and whatever house you enter, first say, 'Peace be to this house.' … and stay in that house eating and drinking what they give you, for the laborer is worthy of his wages. … And whatever city you enter, and they receive you, eat what is set before you" (Luke 10:4-8).

Why did Jesus advocate such austerity for these 70 followers? He obviously wanted them to discover the harvest principle. That would be impossible if they took adequate provisions with them. His teaching aim is stated in Luke 10:2, "The harvest is plentiful but the laborers are few." The hindrance to the Great Commission has never been inadequate financial resources. All the financial resources are provided in the harvest itself. Jeff Christopherson offers some very practical guidelines for applying the harvest principle when planting a new church in his book, *Kingdom First*.[23]

Hindrances to the harvest

Hindrances to achieving the Great Commission focus on the laborers. They have not been sent. Men and women who could gather the crops remain in the barns and grain bins rearranging the yield of past harvests while the future crops rot in the field. Too many churches are afraid of releasing their members to missions, afraid of a weakened home base with lagging budgets and attendance. Too quickly, too easily and too often a "save the institution" outlook suffocates the adventurous missions spirit.

Many lay persons would readily respond to sacrificial missions if leaders would boldly issue the call. Until that happens there will be no national or worldwide awakening. Until then, the harvest will be neglected for want of workers. Jesus' parable about the hiring of laborers at every hour of the day is evidence of His constant search for those who will gather the harvest into His storehouse.

The church has not seen its resources through the eyes of God. The church trembles and says, "Our resources are small and the need is so great. How can our little bit make any difference?" Church budgets are already strained. To plant another church seems out of the question. But, when a concerted effort is made to meet a definite need the resources are multiplied. Is this lesson not at the heart of Jesus' feeding the 5,000 and the 4,000? His power to multiply resources becomes evident when someone is willing to sacrifice a few loaves of bread and a few fish. In faithful obedience to the Lord's command, God's people fed the hungry crowd and a surplus of 12 baskets full were gathered when it was over.

---

[23] Jeff Christopherson, *op.cit.* chapter 9 "Contextual Sustainability.""

Risk in the harvest

Jesus includes risk in the harvest in His statement, "The harvest is plentiful, but the laborers are few, therefore beseech the Lord of the harvest to send out laborers into his harvest. Go your ways, I send you out as lambs in the midst of wolves" (Luke 10:2-3).

Jesus clearly taught the 70 that their task would involve risk. These 70 would embark upon their journey into strange villages without purse, bag or shoes; in today's terms, they were sent without cash, credit cards, cell phone, transportation or contacts for lodging. They began their journey penniless, trusting only in the counsel of Jesus that the resource would be found in the harvest.

Laborers must be sent. That still includes risk today. Without church leaders and laity who are risk-takers, the harvest will remain in the fields and multitudes will enter eternity without Christ.

Churches must give sacrificially, then trust God for multiplication of their resources. Churches must be willing to risk everything rather than seeking their own survival. Jesus said, "For whoever wishes to save his life will lose it; but whoever loses his life for My sake will find it" (Matt. 16:25). This principle that holds true for the individual believer also holds true for the church.

On January 13, 1982, the ill-fated Air Florida flight 90 began its take off from Washington's National Airport. The scream of straining jet engines cold be heard as the aircraft shuddered in a desperate attempt to lift its ice-ladened fuselage. Carrying 79 passengers, it plunged into the icy waters of the Potomac River. As a rescue helicopter returned repeatedly to recover survivors from the deadly cold waters, America witnessed a heroic display of sacrifice. The life ring tethered to the helicopter was thrown to Arland Williams, a 46-year-old bank examiner, but he passed it to another.

Having pulled that passenger from the water, the rescue helicopter returned in minutes to throw the life ring once again to Williams. Although visibly weakening in the freezing water, he passed the ring to someone else.

Returning a third time, the crew searched for the familiar form. Officer Gene Windsor, one of the two-man helicopter rescue crew wept as they described their experience. "He could have gone on the first trip," stated the pilot Donald Usher, "but he put everyone else ahead of himself. Everyone." The blades of the chopper rippled the water with its icy wind. The vision of that empty surface sent chills of awe and sadness through the hearts of millions.

The kind of sacrifice exhibited by Arland Williams must capture the heart of the church. Christians of the 21st century must turn their backs on survivalist instincts and labor sacrificially if the people of the world are to be saved.

On January 23, 1999, Graham Staines, an Australian missionary to India, was burned to death along with his two sons, Philip, age 10, and Timothy, age 6. Staines was 57. For 35 years Graham had ministered to lepers in a remote tribal village in India where he established the Mayurbanj Leprosy Home in 1982. In 1983 he married his wife, Gladys, who joined him in the work.

The mob that killed Graham Staines and his sons was apparently a hardline Hindu organization intent on retribution for the missionary's effectiveness in converting members of the lower caste to faith in Jesus Christ. After the attack, Gladys Staines forgave those who murdered her husband and sons. She remained in India with their daughter, Esther, and continued their ministry among the lepers. She stated, "I cannot just leave those people who love and trust us. I have high regard for the people of India and their tolerance."

The government of India awarded Gladys Staines the fourth highest civilian award in 2005, the *Padma Sri* in recognition for her outstanding contribution to India. She has been called the best known Christian in India after Mother Theresa. In 2015 she was awarded the Mother Theresa Memorial Award for Social Justice.

Their story was made into a movie entitled *The Least of These* and released into theaters on February 1, 2019.   It is a gripping reminder of the cost paid by followers of Christ in every generation and the power of God's love through Jesus Christ.   According to Christianity Today "215 million Christians experience high, very high or extreme levels of persecution."

As in the First Century, the one who said, "So send I you," sends us out as "lambs in the midst of wolves." No risk and no cost is too great for the expansion of the Kingdom.

Importance of Laity in the Harvest

When I arrived in Minnesota-Wisconsin in 1993, the Convention had a tradition of hosting an evangelism conference attended mostly by pastors who listened to other pastors preach. About 50 people showed up.

A couple of years later, we ditched the evangelism conference and decided to replace it with a meeting that would focus on the laity. We enlisted a task force to plan it, composed almost entirely of lay members from the churches. If it was going to be for the laity, we felt the laity should plan it. We only suggested they call it the "Congress on the Laity." Their first action was to discard our suggestion. They said they didn't like anything that dealt with "congress." Instead they chose the term "Empower".

We reserved the Green Lake Baptist Conference Center in Green Lake, Wisconsin and challenged entire families to come at their own expense for three days. The venue included break-out conferences for lay involvement in Kingdom service. Over 800 showed up: Anglo, African American, Hmong, Hispanic and others including all ages.

In the English vernacular we use the term layman to refer to an amateur. If we are speaking with medical, legal or technical professionals we ask them to put it in "layman's" terms. But the term carries a different meaning for followers of Christ. The term laity comes from the Greek word, "*laos*" meaning "people." It is the term Peter uses in 1 Peter 2:9. "But you are a chosen race, a royal priesthood, a holy nation, a *people* for God's own possession, that you may proclaim the excellencies of Him who has called you out of darkness into His marvelous light."

This is the root from which we derive our doctrine of the "priesthood of the believer." There is no distinction between clergy and laity. Those who are called to be apostles, prophets, evangelists, pastors and teachers (Eph. 4:11) are not called to a "higher" position of hierarchy in the body of Christ. These are support and service positions for the laity, the *people* of God, for the "equipping of the saints for the work of service, to the building up of the body of Christ."

My wife is a career public school teacher. Having earned a teaching degree and a masters in early childhood development, she taught at every level: kindergarten, third grade, secondary education. Her last assignment was a dropout prevention program in the public school system with pregnant and parenting teens. She worked primarily with high school girls who became pregnant. She also worked with some of their boyfriends who fathered the child.

Her task was to teach them how to have a healthy pregnancy, a healthy birth, how to be a parent, stay in school and have a future. When her students learned I was a pastor, they exclaimed, "Miss! You're married to a preacher and you're teaching us this!" Her girls achieved a 98% graduation rate, most of them African American and Hispanic. Some had never ventured outside their neighborhood in Garland, Texas. She took them on field trips to colleges and trade schools introducing them to possibilities to advance their educations.

In 2005 Hurricane Rita struck Houston. It was the most intense tropical cyclone ever recorded in the Gulf of Mexico. Many fled inland, including one of her former students who had graduated and moved to the Houston area. When she arrived in Garland, she returned to my wife's class to visit. On that same day a high school counselor dropped by the class to observe. My wife asked her former student to tell her story as an encouragement to the others.

She related the fact that her brother had committed suicide, jumping from the Lake Ray Hubbard Bridge when he was a student. As an unwed teenage mother she realized her life was headed for the same disastrous end. But she was able to graduate, attend a trade school and had a successful career in Houston. The counselor asked the girl what made the difference in her life. She quietly pointed at my wife and said, "This woman right here."

Later, when my wife was diagnosed with breast cancer we went to Baylor Hospital in Dallas to meet with her doctor. Afterward she insisted we visit one of her students who had given birth to a baby. We found the room. The girl was there, along with her boyfriend, the baby's father. They were alone. The baby had died at birth. She had a picture of the newborn baby on the nightstand beside her bed. I was able to tell her I was a pastor and pray with this young heart-broken couple.

My wife, like all laity, was front line. I simply supported and encouraged her.

Church planting is not about programs or gimmicks. Church planting is about empowering the laity to make a difference in the lives of those around them.

Churches and the Harvest

The Scripture teaches sacrificial living with its ultimate expression in the life and death of Jesus. But many churches turn inward and focus on their own survival. The principles that govern individual faith are the principles that bring life and death to the corporate body of Christ. When the church turns inward and is more concerned with survival than sacrifice, it is courting decline and death. From the core, it begins to rot. The thrill of commitment is lost. Motivation for outreach becomes distorted as church visitors and new residents are seen as "prospects" for financial support and perpetuation of the institution. The church turns its attention to unclaimed members of the denomination in hopes that their tithes and energy will help the church survive.

Every church must embrace its death. A church that risks its own survival to sponsor another church sets in motion an interesting dynamic. Life within the new mission becomes contagious. Soon the sponsor church is experiencing new life and a new vision.

Churches must risk all in order to win some. They must refocus their vision on the waves of wheat ready for harvest!

Questions to consider:

1. Is our church more concerned about survival or kingdom expansion?
2. Does our church seek to reach people to strengthen the church, or does it seek to meet the spiritual needs of people?
3. What resources does our church have to assist in starting a new church?
4. How much of our church's resources would be required to start a new church?
5. Would God provide the resources for church starting through people reached by that effort?
6. Is our church willing to take the risk necessary for starting a new church?
7. Are there people in our church who would be willing to form the core of a new church?
8. Am I willing to take the risk to help start a new church?

CHAPTER EIGHT

LEADERSHIP

"You are Peter, and upon this rock I will build my church" (Matt. 16:18). Perhaps no statement by Jesus has been more critically examined or had more influence over the progress of Christian history. The Catholic Church has turned to this statement across the centuries for "Petrine Supremacy," that Jesus established the basis for Papal infallibility when he identified Peter as the rock upon which His church would be built.

This conclusion is quickly dismissed by the fact that within a matter of moments Jesus is rebuking Peter, saying, "Get behind me, Satan! You are a stumbling block to me; for you are not putting your mind on God's interests, but man's" (Matt. 16:23).

Identification of the Pope as the successor of Peter dates back to Cyprian in 256. But prior to that time, and especially in the first century, no such understanding existed. In fact, the Book of Acts clearly affirms the importance of Peter's role, but falls far short of making him a "pope" with the power of making infallible decrees. The Jerusalem council, convened in Acts 15, limits Peter's participation to that of a witness. James, Jesus' half-brother, moderated the meeting and drafted the conclusions of the assembly that was sent to Antioch and the emerging churches where non-Jews were trusting Christ. Peter had an important role and enormous influence, but he was no pope.

Jesus' word for Peter, *petros,* is a Greek word in the masculine gender meaning "rock." Jesus chose the neuter, *petra,* to describe the rock upon which He would build His church. Here, as on other occasions, Jesus used a play on words to make a concept stick in the minds of his followers.

The rock cliffs of Caesarea Philippi likely formed a backdrop for Jesus' statement. He had taken his disciples to this distant place near the border of Syria to prepare them for the crucifixion that would soon follow. He referred to the *petra,* or rock, upon which he would build his church while standing in the shadow of these cliffs where pagan worship had taken place for centuries. The object of his reference is clearly Peter's confession: "You are the Christ, the Son of the living God" (Matt. 16:16). It is upon this confession of faith and the truth of His identity that Jesus would build His church. As He predicted to the woman at the well in Samaria, His followers would worship in spirit and in truth.

But, we must not dismiss entirely the implications of Jesus' reference to Peter. Peter was important. Leadership is important, and Peter had clearly emerged as the leader among the twelve. In every age, in every place and in every church, leadership makes a difference. More than buildings, location, population, history and tradition, leaders determine the future of a congregation. Examples are everywhere.

Leaders Who Made a Difference

Leith Anderson

Leith Anderson became good friends when we lived in Minnesota where he served as senior pastor at Wooddale Church in the 1990s.

In 1943 a group of students and adults came together for Bible study in Richfield, Minnesota and formed the Wayside Chapel. Six years later the Chapel renamed itself Wooddale Baptist Church and joined the Baptist General Conference. Wooddale Baptist grew to 200 in attendance and built a traditional building. They remained at that number until 1977 when they called Leith Anderson as their pastor.

Transition wasn't easy. But over the next 35 years Leith Anderson led the small congregation to relocate to 32 acres, construct a contemporary worship complex and start nine new churches. Wooddale grew to more than 3,000 average attendance with a global reach for missions. When Leith retired from Wooddale in 2011 he was named president of the National Association of Evangelicals.

Stuart Briscoe

In 1958 30 people met at Leland Elementary school in Elm Grove, Wisconsin and formed First Baptist Church of Brookfield, a suburb of Milwaukee. In 1964 the church moved into its first building and changed its name to Elmbrook Baptist Church. Over the next four years the churched changed its name again to Elmbrook Church and built a 450-seat auditorium. In 1970, they invited Stuart Briscoe to serve as their senior pastor.

Briscoe was 40 years old, a well-known evangelist. His friends warned him not to accept the invitation. Milwaukee was well known as an "evangelical graveyard." They told him it would be the end of his career. He accepted anyway.

Over the next 30 years Stuart Briscoe led the church to purchase 39 acres of land and build a worship complex. The church grew to more than 7,000 attendance, the largest in Wisconsin and one of the 100 largest churches in the United States. By 2000 Elmbrook had planted nine additional churches in the Milwaukee area and supported 150 missionaries world-wide.

When I moved to Minnesota in 1993 Stuart agreed to visit with me. I asked him about his secret to success in the Milwaukee area. He said most who lived there were Catholic or Lutheran. If you asked them if they were a Christian, they would say yes.

But, he said, if you asked them if they were a disciple, they would say no. Once he explained that Jesus never referred to his followers as Christians, but always referred to them as disciples, he would explain what it meant to be a disciple of Jesus. They focused on making disciples.

Tom Nelson and Mel Sumrall

In the mid-1980s I served as director of missions for the Denton Baptist Association in Denton, Texas. I knew that Denton Bible Church existed, but it was not very visible. When I drove east on Highway 380 I passed the site where the church was located near Texas Woman's University. It was hidden behind a grove of trees. With its poor visibility and access, I thought it would never grow. I was wrong. Twenty years later Denton Bible Church surpassed 3,500 in attendance. Today it occupies an impressive campus on Highway 380 and sponsors 49 missionary families serving around the world.

The leadership that produced Denton Bible Church involves two men, Mel Sumrall and Tom Nelson. Mel was called into the ministry when he was 48. He left a successful business in southern Colorado, moved to Texas and started Denton Bible Church in 1976 with 14 people meeting in a renovated fire station. The next year Mel added Tom Nelson as Associate Pastor. The two formed a rare leadership team combining age and youth, vision and teaching. The church grew. God gave the increase. Their story is beautifully told on the church website.[24]

In the late 1990s, when our family had moved to Minnesota, our oldest son enrolled at the University of North Texas and came under the discipleship of Denton Bible Church. In 2019 he still benefits from pastor Tom Nelson's teaching. Our son

---

[24] https://dentonbible.org/about-us/history-of-dbc/

leads Bible studies for high school students in Sundance, Wyoming. More than 50% of the student body attend.

Steve Stroope Lake Pointe, Rockwall

I first met Steve Stroop in 1979. He had been serving as youth pastor at a church in Dallas. My good friend, JV Thomas had led the First Baptist Church of Rockwall, Texas to sponsor a new church across the water on Lake Ray Hubbard in Rowlett. They launched Dalrock Baptist Church in a marina on the lake and called Steve to serve as their pastor. That was 40 years ago.

Within a year Steve led the church to purchase land and build a first unit building. It was identical to the building we had built in The Colony a year before. When Steve led the church to relocate to Rockwall they changed the name to Lake Pointe. Jackie and I joined Lake Pointe in 2001 and were members for 10 years. During that time the church grew from 6,000 to more than 10,000 with satellite congregations in Mesquite, Forney, Garland and Richardson in addition to the main campus in Rockwall, Texas.

Lake Pointe is involved in missions world-wide with 40 new church plants and 18 international partners.

Jimmy Seibert Antioch Church, Waco, Texas

Jimmy Seibert grew up in Beaumont, Texas without attending church. But, as a sophomore in high school he began to ask the question, "Is God real?" Through his brother, Dave, and a few friends, God answered. He gave his life to Christ, but, without anyone to disciple him, his spiritual growth was slow.

God spoke to Jimmy in a dream. Life cannot be lived on the fence. It took several years for him to realize what that meant, but one summer during his college years, he got off the fence, wholly committed his life to follow Jesus, and everything changed. Jesus made Himself real. He began a new journey.

As college pastor at Highland Baptist Church in Waco, Texas, Jimmy was instrumental in launching "Master's Commission" and "World Mandate." The ministry multiplied, moved beyond Highland Baptist Church, began launching churches world-wide in 1993 and launched Antioch Church in Waco in 1999. In the last 20 years hundreds of missionaries have been sent to the ends of the earth through the Antioch movement and scores of churches have been started following "a passion for Jesus and His purposes in the earth." Jimmy Seibert tells the story in his book, *Passion & Purpose*. Antioch, Waco, averages over 3,000 at their home campus.

Since 2009 our daughter, Allison, and her husband Noah have served on staff with Antioch, first as Children's Pastor at Antioch, Waco and more recently as Executive Pastor of Antioch Church, Fort Collins, Colorado.

Bob Roberts, Northwood, Keller

I met Bob Roberts in the mid-1980s. He was an ambitious young pastor in Fort Worth opposed to church planting. We met again a few years later. Not only was he interested in church planting, he was planting a new church, Northwood Church in Keller, Texas. He invited me to preach for him in the local high school where they were meeting for temporary space. That was almost 30 years ago. He grew Northwood to become one of the leading churches in the nation with a reputation for serving those with special needs. He also led Northwoods to embrace the nations. Northwood focuses on mobilizing believers to serve their communities and the world through their vocations. In 2004 I accompanied Bob and several other pastors to visit Egypt as guests of the Egyptian Embassy. Bob is one of the most gifted and visionary leaders I have ever known.

Northwood practices *glocal* missions. " A key word in Northwood's vocabulary is glocal (global + local). We feel it is important for our members to take their faith outside our church walls and make an impact for Jesus Christ in our community and around the world. We serve others using our jobs, our skills and our passions."[25]

In 2019 Northwood sponsored eleven mission trips to Viet Nam focused on: orphan care/youth, education, medical care, community development, women's ministry, business training, marriage/family, child abuse prevention/medical, and soccer. Northwood has planted over 200 churches in North America. Each year Northwood provides assessment, training, coaching and mentoring to equip up to 25 church planters.

In each of these cases, leadership made the difference.

Church Planters Whose Leadership Is Making a Difference

The examples included above are my contemporaries who proved themselves successful over more than 30 years. Most church planters and pastors will not see the remarkable results that these have experienced. We would err to conclude that effective leadership always results in a mega-church and world-wide missions. Effective leadership is needed in every church, large and small. And it is needed at every stage: planting, development, growth, expansion and multiplication.

My wife and I moved to northern Colorado in 2016. We were happy in Waco, Texas where we were hosting an international Bible study in our home. We had grown to love our

---

[25] https://northwoodchurch.org/about/

internationals as our own kids. But they all graduated and have been scattered to the ends of the earth: Indonesia, South Korea, South Africa, Zambia, Indiana and Texas. They are all making a Kingdom difference.

At the same time, our daughter and son-in-law accepted an invitation to serve as executive pastor at Antioch Church in Fort Collins, Colorado, a new church that is part of the Antioch Movement. They took our two granddaughters with them! And, after moving in 2015, gave birth to our grandson. Our oldest son and daughter-in-law were raising our older grandchildren in Wyoming.

It didn't take a lot of spiritual intuition or prayer to know that the path for our future was, once again, outside Texas. So, we sold our house in Texas and moved to Fort Collins, Colorado. It was more complicated than that, but that was the bottom line.

What we didn't know was that the Lord was doing something special in church planting in northern Colorado, and that He had a place for us. In 2016 John Howeth, NAMB's Church Planter Catalyst for the area, asked me to serve as mentor and coach for church planters. I have grown to love these guys. I am grateful for them and proud of them.

Each is demonstrating leadership in the early stages of giving birth to a new church. Each is unique. Unlike the examples above, we don't know the outcome. But that is the way leadership is exercised. Effective leadership never has the luxury of hindsight. We must lead looking forward into a future that often can resemble a Texas fog or Minnesota white out.

Kelly Parrish grew up in a small town near Lubbock, Texas, and played quarterback at Howard Payne University in Brownwood where he met his wife, Brandi, a Howard Payne cheerleader. After marriage and graduation, he started a career in business. Then God called them to start Living Rock Church in Timnath, Colorado in 2014. They have baptized over 87 and launched two other churches in their first four years. Timnath is adjacent to Fort Collins.

AJ Neely also grew up in Texas and graduated from Texas A&M. After serving as youth pastor in several churches, God called AJ and his wife Holly to Loveland, Colorado to start a church. Several families relocated with them from their home church in Arlington, Texas. After a year of internship with Kelly in Timnath, they launched in January 2019 with 90 present and average 70 in High Plains Elementary School. Loveland is 10 miles south of Fort Collins.

Josh Green served in the police force in Tyler, Texas for 20 years. Before he retired God called him to revitalize a small church in Bullard, Texas as a bi-vocational pastor. In 2017 God led Josh and his wife Amy to start a new church in Severance, Colorado. After one year as intern with Kelly Parrish, they launched Living Rock Severance on January 13, 2019 with 167. They average 130. Severance is 10 miles east of Fort Collins.

Zack Thurman grew up in Tacoa, Georgia. After God called him into the ministry he served as executive pastor at Buck Run Baptist Church in Frankfort, Kentucky. God called Zack and his wife Jennifer to Fort Collins in 2017. They launched Overland Church in January 2019 averaging more than 100 in a building that was donated to them.

John Richardson grew up in Mississippi and helped start a student church in San Francisco while attending seminary. He and his wife, JD returned to Mississippi and started a campus-based church in Clinton. They transitioned from this church and served with Generous Church, a stewardship ministry, before sensing another call to church planting. After exploring several possibilities, they were called to Wellington, Colorado in 2015. Trailhead Church launched in January 2016. They are now averaging more 150 in three services including Saturday night. Easter attendance in 2019 exceeded 400. They are planning to sponsor two new churches in 2019 including a Hispanic congregation. Wellington is 10 miles north of Fort Collins.

Bruce Hendrich is in his 60s. He grew up on a wheat farm in Eastern Colorado where his brother still lives. After graduating high school he went to Moody Bible Institute in Chicago and stayed in the area to serve as a pastor. In 2015 God called Bruce and his wife to return to Colorado to start a new church. After one year as an intern at Living Rock Church, Timnath, they launched Grandview Baptist Church in Mead. They baptized 13 in their first year and average more than 90 in attendance. Meade is town of 5,000 people half-way between Denver and Fort Collins.

Oscar de la Cruz, Sr. grew up Catholic with disdain for evangelical Christians. As a young man he and his friends threw rocks at an evangelical church during their worship service. The congregation continued singing hymns of praise as rocks smashed the windows. Oscar was deeply moved and convicted. A a result, he came to faith in Christ. For the past 30 years, Oscar Salazar has been starting churches in Colorado. His son serves as pastor of a church he started in Greely. He is working with John Richardson in Wellington to start another new Hispanic church in 2019.

I do not know what the future holds for these men and the churches they have launched in northern Colorado. But they represent the thousands of leaders God is raising up for the harvest all across North America. On Easter Sunday, 2019, the combined attendance in these new churches, none of which existed five years ago, was more than 1,400.

Characteristics of an Effective Leader

Character

Since I first wrote this book 33 years ago, tons of information, books and conferences have been developed around leadership. In my original manuscript I included a few key characteristics I felt were important. Since that time I have come to believe there is one over-arching, inescapable element that defines effective leadership. That element is character.

We can focus on external actions and characteristics. But character is the one qualifying or disqualifying factor. Character has to do with values: honesty, integrity, truthfulness, humility, thoughtfulness, kindness, compassion, and everything that goes on below the surface: the secret life.

Jesus focused on character. He warned that it is what goes on in the secret places of the heart and mind that ultimately define success or failure. He refers to this in His Sermon on the Mount reminding us repeatedly, "Your Father who sees what is done in secret will reward you" (Matt. 6:4,6,18) It is the central point in his message to the Pharisees: "You clean the outside of the cup and of the platter; but inside of you, you are full of robbery and wickedness" (Luke 11:39). And again, "You are like whitewashed tombs which on the outside appear beautiful, but inside they are full of dead men's bones and all uncleanness" (Mt. 23:27).

As of this writing I am 72 years old. I witnessed Watergate and the Clinton impeachment. You would think that we would have learned our lesson about secrets. President Nixon and "all the President's men" thought that they could get away with it. But every word uttered in the oval office found its way into print and into the public. The Watergate tapes ripped the mask off the public image of politics and left an entire generation disillusioned.

Twenty years later, Bill Clinton assumed that what he did in private would remain secret. But what happened with Monica Lewinsky behind closed doors became public record resulting in the second Presidential impeachment in history. In his autobiography Clinton confessed, "The question of secrets is one I have thought a lot about over the years. ... secrets can be an awful burden to bear, especially if some sense of shame is attached to them ... Of course, I didn't begin to understand all this back when I became a secret-keeper. ...I was always reluctant to discuss with anyone the most difficult parts of my personal life."[26]

We have all been saddened and grieved by the failures of prominent church leaders. Ted Haggard was pastor of New Life Church in Colorado Springs and president of the National Association of Evangelicals before his secret life of gay sex and drugs became public.

Bill Hybels was perhaps the most prominent evangelical leader in America until he resigned Willowcreek Church and Association under charges of sexual harassment and misconduct.

Across the years I have watched many who started ministry with promise end shipwrecked. One church planter in whom I had absolute confidence grew his church to a significant attendance averaging more than 800. But he made headlines when his sexual abuse of a minor became known. The act had remained secret for many years before it was exposed. It destroyed his ministry and damaged the church. Some, as in all such cases, fell away, disillusioned.

---

[26] Clinton, William Jefferson, *Bill Clinton My Life,* (Alfred A. Knopf division of Random House,2004), 46.

This is the reason Paul counseled his young protégé, Timothy, "Fight the good fight, keeping faith and a good conscience, which some have rejected and suffered shipwreck in regard to their faith" (1 Tim. 1:19).

I am happy to say that most of my friends are finishing well in their marriages, their families and their ministry. My wife and I celebrated our 50th anniversary in December, 2018. Most of our friends who devoted themselves to Christian ministry are likewise celebrating life-long marriages. Many have children and grandchildren who have followed them in Christian ministry and service.

That is not to say there have not been heartaches, disappointments and failures along the way. But God is faithful and long suffering. "The lovingkindness of God endures all day long" (Psa. 52:1).

In the short term, leadership can be reduced to identifiable actions. These can be found in many books on the subject. But in the long term, it is all about character. Who are we when we are alone and no one is watching … except God?

Vision and Goals

Jesus' life was driven by vision and goals. When Mary and Joseph were looking for Him in the temple, Jesus' first recorded words declared a sense of priority: "Did you not know I must be about the things of my Father?" (Luke 2:49). Later He responded to Mary's plea for help at the wedding feast in Cana, "My hour has not yet come" (John 2:4). He knew his mission: "The Son of Man is come to seek and save that which was lost" (Luke 19:10).

Not even the prospects of suffering and death clouded his clear vision. "Now my soul is troubled, and what shall I say?

Father, save me from this hour; but for this purpose I came to this hour" (John 12:27).

Nothing could turn Jesus from His goal, not family, friend or foe. He would accomplish the redemptive task for which He had come. His perfect life would be crushed. His spotless soul and spirit would be cast into the depths of hell to pay the penalty for our sins. He willingly gave his life so that guilty men might be spared the consequences of their own sin. His goal was clear.

The Apostle Paul single-mindedly pursued his goal: "This one thing I do, forgetting those things which are behind, and reaching forth unto those things which are before, I press toward the mark for the prize of the high calling of God in Christ Jesus" (Phil. 3:13, 14).

His purpose is further clarified in his statements to the Corinthians: "For I determined not to know anything among you, save Jesus Christ and Him crucified" (1 Cor. 2:2). "I have become all things to all men, so that I may by all means save some" (1 Cor. 9:22).

Whether it is Abraham Lincoln with his unswerving dedication to preserve the Union, or Winston Churchill with his commitment to victory at all costs, or Martin Luther King, Jr. with his dream of racial equality, effective leaders operate with clear concise goals.

Practical Steps

Deliberately and systematically, Jesus began His three-year ministry. He did not move randomly about the countryside passing time until "His hour" should come. Each miracle, each parable, each action, each word was aimed at clarifying for humanity the divine will. Each day, each hour brought Him closer to His purpose which culminated in His death and resurrection.

The Apostle was concerned with his disciplined race to his goal. "Therefore I run in such a way, as not without aim; I box in such a way, as not beating the air" (1 Cor. 9:26). Acts reveals Paul's systematic church planting in major metropolitan areas by entering the synagogues, entering into dialogue with the priests, winning the "God fearers," and establishing a base of operation. While Paul worked, he discipled others to plant churches in other cities.

Effective leaders must be able to design effective plans as well as dream great dreams. Joseph, perhaps the greatest Old Testament dreamer, became Egypt's prime minister after demonstrating an ability to design strategies and organize men to implement those dreams. To be effective the church must have leaders who can take practical steps to accomplish their plans to embrace the world with the gospel.

Communication and Enlistment

A vision locked within a single mind cannot change the world. The idea must be communicated in such a way that it becomes the dream of others. It must be communicated in such practical ways that others will help make that shared dream a reality.

Jesus, the master-leader of men, communicated His dream. Men were willing to leave family, career and possessions to follow in the Kingdom pursuit. Although they did not understand His full strategy, they wanted to join His spiritual revolution.

Paul successfully communicated his goals and dreams. Although his companions at Troas did not receive the Macedonian vision, they were captured by its power once Paul communicated the vision to them. "After he (Paul) had seen the vision, immediately we sought to go into Macedonia, concluding that God had called us to preach the gospel to them" (Act 16:10). As he continued, the list of those challenged by Paul's vision grew to include Timothy, Titus, Silas, Luke, Priscilla, Aquila, Lydia, Justus, Crispus, Jason and Tertius.

For spiritual awakening to sweep the world, God must raise up men with a vision for total world evangelism, men with a grasp for the right methods to accomplish that end and men with the ability to inspire others to follow. Re-writing this book 33 years after its first publication, I am convinced God is doing this very thing.

Taking Risk

Leadership is always risky business. Martin Luther risked defeat and death when he launched the Reformation. He expected to end his life as a martyr. William Carey risked livelihood and safety when he quit his job and left his home to carry the gospel to India. His risk marked the beginning of the modern missionary movement.

Jesus encouraged risk-taking. Through parables he encouraged His disciples to risk all for the pearl of great price, for the treasure hidden in a field, to invest whatever "talents" they had been given so that God could give the increase. Through example He showed His followers how to jeopardize reputation and life for a worthy cause.

Some can dream dreams. They can devise workable plans for accomplishing those dreams. They can motivate others to help make the dreams reality. But without a willingness to risk, these gifted people will never lead.

Questions for pastors and churches:

1. Who is the most effective leader you know? What are his leadership qualities?
2. Does my church have a definite vision and goals for the future?
3. Has my church identified a specific plan to reach its vision and goals?
4. Are members motivated to pursue the vision and goals of our church?
5. Am I willing to take the risks necessary to lead my church?
6. Is our church willing to take the risks necessary to disciple more people?
7. If our church is searching for a pastor, what are the leadership qualities we are looking for?
8. If our church is starting a new church, what kind of leader do we need as pastor?
9. Do lay people in our church possess leadership gifts?
10. How can the leadership qualities of key lay people be enlisted to achieve the vision and goals of our church?

CHAPTER NINE

PLANNING

Jesus' statement to Peter reflects a strategy for warfare when he says of the church, "The gates of Hades shall not overpower it" (Matt. 16:18). Satan is besieged in his fortress of darkness. With supply lines cut off, his retreat blocked, he trembles behind locked doors as battering rams of light pound the gates. It is the climax of the battle.

This imagery evokes visions of a despairing Hitler trapped in his bunker, listening to the relentless pounding of Allied bombs that shook the concrete walls of his underground refuge. The perpetrator of the holocaust did not come to his end accidentally. Years of strategy and coordinated efforts by the Allied forces led to the ultimate defeat of this crazed and powerful ruler who pushed humanity to the brink of destruction.

The church must likewise carry out its onslaught against Satan's kingdom with a coordinated effort employing all its forces in a well-planned strategy for victory. For the church to do otherwise would be disastrous.

Jesus talked in terms of a battle plan in another illustration: "Or what king, when he sets out to meet another king in battle, will not first sit down and consider whether he is strong enough with ten thousand men to encounter the one coming against him with twenty thousand? Or else, while the other is still far away, he sends a delegation and asks for terms of peace" (Luke 14:31-32). He was explaining the necessity to count the cost of discipleship. But he was also teaching the principle of wise planning.

Planning in Paul's Ministry

The Apostle Paul emphasized the importance of planning in his statement to the Corinthians, "according to the grace of God which is given unto me, as a wise master builder, I laid a foundation, and another is building on it" (1 Cor. 3:10).

Paul's choice of words here is important. His words which are translated "wise master builder," *sophos arketekton,* could be translated "wise architect." My older brother and my son are both architects. It took years of study and internship before they were licensed. They must continue to update their license in order to stay current with building materials, best practices and design.

In the architectural profession, each well-executed project requires extensive study and preparation. Building custom homes on steep cliffs, the architect must work to convert rough, unfriendly terrain into a habitable place with aesthetic grace. To plan towering skyscrapers, he must calculate not only the effect of his building upon those surrounding it, but he must consider the effect of those buildings upon his own design.

Utilities, foundation, engineering, appearance, access and egress are planned. Details must be carefully drafted before the first shovel of dirt is turned. Likewise, the *sophos arketekton* of the Kingdom must carefully plan for multiplied and growing churches.

Most of us have little knowledge of what goes into the construction of a building. But all of us know how it feels when we walk in. The architecture communicates to our senses, whether sterile, nostalgic, modern, relaxed or worshipful. We know what we feel when we step into the building, whether a hospital, bank, restaurant, church or home.

In the same way, people can feel the design of your church when they come together. Some of this is communicated by the physical facilities, but more importantly, they feel the character of the people, whether warm, friendly, helpful, welcoming, authentic, or otherwise. How you plan and how you "build" has a lot to do with the result. Others will never know the planning effort you expend to start a church (organization, leadership development, set up, worship, child care, etc.) but they will immediately "feel" the difference.

Acts makes it clear that Paul did not approach church starting haphazardly. Acts 16 reveals the struggle engaged by the Apostle as he sought to develop his strategy. The Scripture simply states, "They passed through the Phrygian and Galatian region, having been forbidden by the Holy Spirit to speak the word in Asia; and after they came to Mysia, they were trying to go into Bithynia, and the Spirit of Jesus did not permit them; and passing by Mysia, they came down to Troas" (Acts 16:6-8). It was there that Paul and his companions received the Macedonian vision that led them into continental Europe, a decision which set the destiny for modern Christianity.

This seems simple but there must have been an agonizing search for the right strategy throughout this experience.

In one way or another, Paul was seeking God's blueprint for missions in the first century world. It is hardly accidental that he would spend his energies establishing "mission base" churches in the metropolitan centers: Philippi, Corinth, Thessalonica and Ephesus.

Acts depicts the broad strokes of the *sophos arketekton*. But careful inspection also reveals exacting details. In each city Paul quickly followed his adopted pattern, seeking those who were spiritually sensitive to revealed truth through the Scriptures. As Jesus had instructed the 70, Paul looked for "persons of peace." He would enter the synagogues and speak

111

first to the Jews. But his greatest response was from the "God fearers," those Gentiles who had adopted the God of Abraham, Isaac and Jacob. These became his nuclei for reaching the multitudes of the Gentile world through the successful multiplication of Gentile Christian churches. This was his plan of action for reaching the Roman world.

Planning in the Early Church

Paul was not the first to employ strategies for growth and effectiveness. Acts 6:1-7 gives a remarkable insight into the planning process adopted by the church soon after Pentecost. This account of choosing the first deacons begins and ends with two strong statements of growth. Acts 6:1 opens the passage with this statement: "Now at this time while the number of disciples was increasing, a complaint arose ..." Acts 6:7 closes the passage: "The number of disciples continued to increase greatly in Jerusalem ... "

The intervening verses found in Acts 6:2-6 imply that growth for the Jerusalem church had reached a plateau. Some imbalance in the evangelistic outreach and internal ministry was hindering the multiplication of disciples. In one of the most dramatic moments in Scripture, the church paused to seek a solution to this dilemma so that once again the number of disciples might be multiplied.

The manner in which these early church leaders handled the problem is instructive to churches in the 21st Century. In very clear fashion they adopted methods for problem solving that can work in any context.

Establish a Small Leadership Group

At this early stage, the leadership group in the rapidly growing church at Jerusalem consisted of the eleven plus Matthias. In fact, their first "order of business" was to replace Judas so that their "leadership group" was complete (Acts 1:15-26). This does not imply that every new church needs a core leadership of 12. For most new churches that would be a huge number. But every new church needs a small group of recognized leaders who can make decisions.

When I first wrote this book in 1986, many new churches were launched without any core leadership team. In many cases, the church planter was "it." Fortunately this has been corrected in most church planting efforts today. Many launch with a board of elders including members from the sponsoring congregation. Others launch with a small group of elders who make up the church planting team prior to launch. There are other methods and designs, but having a small group of mature believers with good wisdom and judgment who come alongside the church planter for decision making is vital to the success of a church plant.

Identify Any Obstacle to Making Disciples

In Acts 6, this group apparently met together and identified a present threat to the health and success of the Jerusalem church. They had been growing rapidly since Pentecost, holding all things in common, ministering to one another in the "daily distribution of bread." But the growth was slowing. The logistics of the early systems that sustained the first days following Pentecost were breaking down. The number of disciples being added daily was slowing. The church was in danger of chugging to a stop, becoming bound up with internal issues and losing its cutting edge for making disciples.

So they met and discussed the situation. This happened somewhere between Acts 6:1 and 6:2. Often we have to read between the lines in Scripture to understand what is happening "behind the scenes." The Twelve could not have summoned the congregation and given their report if they had not met

113

prior to the summons. This must have been an interesting meeting.

Perhaps the consensus was immediate. Maybe they were all aware of the problem they were facing before they sat down. At any rate, once they got together, the issue was clear. A discontent was growing within the body of new believers. The Hellenistic Jews felt their widows were being overlooked in the daily distribution of food and the Jewish widows were getting favorable treatment. Of course this was long before the circumcision controversy that led to the Jerusalem Council debate in Acts 15. These were "God fearing" Greek believers who had previously converted to Judaism before becoming followers of Jesus, the Messiah.

So, they faced the question, "What do we do about it?"

Consider Solutions

All of the Twelve were Jews. It is significant that apparently they took the complaint seriously and sought an answer. Whether or not the Greek widows were neglected was not the issue. The issue was that they felt neglected.

One solution they considered was to work harder. I have often thought Peter might have put this option forward. He seems to have always been full of energy, ready to get up an hour early and work an hour late to get the job done. However it came, the group dismissed it as unworkable.

This kind of thinking is all too often present in new churches. With every additional challenge the church planter and core leaders work a little harder, adding one additional thing to their plate. Before long they are facing burn out. I am pleased that contemporary church planters appear to do better at this than my generation 40 years ago.

Each additional challenge is an opportunity to delegate responsibility and tasks. Usually those who must assume the task are less equipped and perhaps not as gifted as the church planting team, but they will grow and they will learn. We must trust people to do the job, even if it is not up to our standards. They can, and usually will, improve.

The Apostles must have faced this same dilemma. No one could take care of the Greek-speaking widows as well as they could. Their assessment that they should not neglect prayer and the Word focuses on their value for "Sabbath" disciplines. Too often church planters become so busy with the many tasks required to start a church that they neglect to nourish their souls.

Several years after we started a church in 1976 I realized I was preaching twice on Sunday morning, again on Sunday evening, teaching a Bible study on Wednesday evening and writing a weekly devotional column for the local newspaper. I was spending a lot of time in Bible study. But the Lord convicted me that all of my Bible study was focused on finding something to say to someone else, in the pulpit, in a Bible study or in my column. I made a covenant with the Lord that I would spend time in devotional Bible reading, taking notes on what the Lord said specifically to me. My covenant included a commitment that I would not use whatever the Lord said to me in a sermon or Bible study. It would be a personal conversation just between God and me. I had to change all the pronouns from second and third person to first. God wanted to speak to me, not to someone else. It changed the course of my life. I still had to prepare for sermons, Bible study and writing, but what God wanted to say to me in my personal devotional time was private. This was a difficult discipline.

Pray

The fact that the Apostles refused to neglect the Word of God and prayer indicates that prayer was essential to all they did. Surely as they considered solutions to the immediate problem, they spent time in prayer.

They had learned this from Jesus. He prayed all night before he selected the Twelve. He rose long before daylight, sought a solitary place and prayed. He taught his disciples to pray. Everything He did was connected to prayer and what he saw the Father doing.

I have never met anyone who said they prayed too little. When Billy Graham reached the final years of his life, after he had preached to more than 200 million people in 185 countries he said he wished he had spent more time in prayer.

We are all on a journey with God. We cannot rely solely on our own intelligence or intuition. We need the guidance of the Holy Spirit in all we do. We must not neglect prayer. We must not proceed without it.

Involve the Entire Congregation

The proposed solution involved delegation.

"Therefore, brethren, select from among you seven men of good reputation, full of the Spirit and of wisdom, whom we may put in charge of this task. But we will devote ourselves to prayer and to the [d]ministry of the word" (Acts 6:3-4).

Not only would they place others over this task, they would trust the congregation to help them identify the persons to do the job. They not only reported to the congregation, they included them in the solution. They were clear about the qualifications, but they would trust their fellow believers to choose the men to assume this task.

Acts 6 describes a beautiful process in which the leaders and the church worked together to create a new ministry within the body, "The statement found approval with the whole congregation; and they chose Stephen, a man full of faith and of the Holy Spirit, and Philip, Prochorus, Nicanor, Timon, Parmenas and Nicolas, a proselyte from Antioch. And these they brought before the apostles; and after praying, they laid their hands on them" (Acts 6:5-6).

The Apostles clearly identified the problem within the Jerusalem body of believers, reported why they had come to the conclusion they presented, then asked the church to join them in filling these positions. After they were selected, the Apostles commissioned them with authority and responsibility for the task.

Implement the Proposed Strategy

Many good strategies gather dust from neglect. Churches have often adopted well-designed projects only to have their dreams fade, phantom-like, in a fog of procrastination. Unless strategies are implemented, the entire process remains futile.

The Jerusalem church implemented its strategy. The Apostles practiced delegation of authority and ministry to these seven while the people accepted the care extended by these chosen lay leaders. These seven began their ministry to the Greek-speaking widows.

The importance of this action in the fledgling body of believers in Jerusalem cannot be overestimated. It set the course for the future of the church. All of the men who were chosen by the Jerusalem church for this ministry have Greek names. They were "God Fearers," Greek converts to Judaism who became followers of Jesus, the Messiah. They were uniquely equipped to perform the immediate task, serving the Greek-speaking widows. But they were also uniquely equipped to launch the church into areas the Twelve could not have anticipated.

Besides caring for the widows, Stephen proceeded to preach boldly. Like Jesus, he was dragged before the Council and confronted by the High Priest. But, unlike Jesus, Stephen did not remain silent. Instead he delivered a dramatic review of Israel's rebellion against the prophets and their greatest crime, murdering the "Righteous One" (Acts 7). Outraged, they immediately stoned Stephen to death while a young Pharisee named Saul looked on.

This led to a widespread persecution in Jerusalem, with the result that the believers all scattered, except the Apostles. The seven, who had been chose to wait on tables, became the leaders of this diaspora that spread the gospel to Samaria (Acts 8) and carried the gospel to Antioch (Acts 11:19) where a church was planted that would become the sending church for Paul's journeys. The reference to Nicholas as a "proselyte from Antioch" cannot be coincidental.

God's plans often far exceed our own.

Evaluate the Results

Here is their evaluation statement: "The Word of God increased and the number of disciples in Jerusalem multiplied greatly; and a great company of priests were obedient to the faith" (Acts 6:7). It is interesting to note that they evaluated the results in terms of their core value: to make disciples. They did not say, "And the Greek-speaking widows were cared for and ceased to complain." That might have been the case, but their chief concern was to keep their focus on making disciples.

While churches seldom gather enough information to analyze alternatives, and fewer churches implement what they design, only rarely do churches take the time to evaluate the results of their actions. Adopted programs and strategies continue without consideration for their effectiveness.

Without evaluation, initial problems may continue unsolved or be compounded by partial cures. Programing without evaluation can easily focus the energy of the church on side issues that fall short of its primary task.

Bold planning must be rediscovered if the church is to carry out Jesus' Great Commission. This is the key that unlocks the door to catalytic missions, the essential element that produces a chain reaction of multiplied churches and disciples.

A few churches will start around a catalytic individual who starts a church on his own initiative. Others will take place from the natural splits that occur within congregations. But the number of these churches will be relatively small. Seldom will inroads be made beyond the dominant cultural or language group in which the existing church or denomination has its roots.

Penetration of the population will dwindle as unchurched minorities outstrip the immigration and birth rates of European Americans. Generational dropouts will increase among the previously churched. Secularism will continue to spread as the biological growth of the church falters behind that of the world. A spiritually illiterate generation will replace its devout forebears.

Only by adopting the planning process of the First Century church will we regain the offensive and aggressively attack the fortress of darkness. Those who lift up their eyes to the fields, analyze the nature of the harvest, design appropriate strategies, then enter the harvest with indefatigable commitment will find themselves participating in church planting movements that relive the book of Acts.

Questions for discussion:

1. Has growth stopped in our church? Are we growing year-to-year?
2. What are the possible obstacles that could be preventing our church from growing?
3. What are some possible solutions to overcome these obstacles to growth?
4. What is the best solution?
5. How can we involve the people of our church in finding possible hindrances to growth and overcoming them?
6. Has our church implemented strategic proposals in the past?
7. Are there programs and activities in our church that need evaluation?
8. Are there sections of the population around us that are not being reached by our church or other churches?
9. How can our church reach these unreached population groups?
10. Does our church need to sponsor the plant of a new church in our area?

About the Author

Bill and Jackie Tinsley

Bill Tinsley has served as pastor and missions leader in Texas, Minnesota and Wisconsin. His experience includes sixteen years as a pastor, seven years as Director of Missions for Denton Baptist Association, Denton, Texas, eight years as Executive Director for Minnesota-Wisconsin Baptist Convention and two years as Associate Executive Director of the Baptist General Convention of Texas. He led WorldconneX from 2003-2009, an organization designed to explore missions innovation in the 21st century.

He has international experience in South America, Africa, Asia, Australia and Europe. In 2012 he and his wife, Jackie, served as interim pastor for the International Baptist Church in Nuremberg, Germany.

Bill has written fourteen books and writes a weekly faith column currently carried in newspapers nationwide and syndicated by Gatehouse Media. His blog has received more than 130,000 views worldwide including Russia, Germany, UK, Canada, Slovenia, Netherlands, Poland, Philippines, India and China. (www.reflectionscolumns.blogspot.com)

He created The Tinsley Center in 2010 to develop authentic disciples who impact their community and the world for Christ. (www.tinsleycenter.com). Since 2012 he has led Peer Learning groups for pastors in Minnesota and Wisconsin. He has coached church planters in Colorado since 2016.

He and his wife, Jackie celebrated their 50th anniversary December 21, 2018. They have three children and six grandchildren. They make their home in Fort Collins, Colorado.

Web site: www.tinsleycenter.com
Email william.tinsley@sbcglobal.net

Other Books by William (Bill) Tinsley

The Jesus Encounter Stories of people in the Bible who met Jesus., paperback Veritas Publishing 2000, hardback Zondervan 2002. How would people like Nicodemus, Zacchaeus, Mary Magdalene and others describe their encounter with Jesus? Email william.tinsleys@sbcglobal.net for copies.)

Finding God's Vision: Missions and the New Realities Veritas Publishing 2005. Amazon eBook.
Seven ways God is reshaping the world for His purposes.

The Authentic Disciple, Meditations in Mark, Veritas Publishing 2002. Devotions from the Gospel of Mark. Available on Amazon as eBook and paperback.

Authentic Disciple: Sermon On the Mount February Tinsley Center 2010. Devotions from the Sermon on the Mount. Available on Amazon as eBook and paperback.

Buddy the Floppy Ear Corgi, Tinsley Center 2010, Children's book that teaches children to love themselves and others just the way God made them. Available on Amazon as eBook and paperback.

Sunrise Sunset Poems, Tinsley Center 2011. Collection of inspirational poems.Available at Amazon as an eBook and in paperback.

People Places and Things, Poems by William Tinsley, Tinsley Center 2011. Collection of award winning poems by Bill Tinsley Available on Amazon as eBook and paperback.

Bold Springs, Tinsley Center 2014. Historical fiction. A Civil War novel. Available on Amazon as ebook and paperback.

Our Story, Bill and Jackie Tinsley. 1968-2018. Tinsley Center 2018. Bill and Jackie Tinsley celebrated their fiftieth anniversary December 21, 2018. This is their story. Available on Amazon as eBook and paperback.

Reflections Vol 1, 2009-2012 Tinsley Center 2016. Collection of faith columns appearing in newspapers and online. Bill Tinsley reflects on current events and life experience from a faith perspective. Reflections have appeared in newspapers nation-wide since 2009. Syndicated by Gatehouse Media. More than 130,000 views online. An Amazon eBook.
To receive current Reflections columns for free, go to www.tinsleycenter.com and subscribe.